Landmark
BOOKS

FERDINAND MAGELLAN

THE FAIR BREEZE BLEW, THE WHITE FOAM FLEW
THE FURROW FOLLOWED FREE:
WE WERE THE FIRST THAT EVER BURST
INTO THAT SILENT SEA.

FERDINAND MAGELLAN

Master Mariner

BY SEYMOUR GATES POND

Illustrated by JACK COGGINS

RANDOM HOUSE · NEW YORK

Contents

FERDINAND MAGELLAN

1

The sailing of the ships

"All ship's company aboard! All ship's company aboard!" The Portuguese master-at-arms, black cape whipping in the night wind, was striding along Lisbon's stone quay ringing his sailing bell vigorously. The low hush of voices increased in tempo. Last-minute farewells were being interspersed with lingering kisses for the departing sailors, many of whom would never see their homes again. Women wept. Hearts beat faster.

Seamen with duffel bags and gifts from loved ones hurried up the rude gangplanks.

Overhead, the stars gleamed brilliantly beyond the mast-tops of Captain-General Almeida's great fleet of twenty-two ships. It was March of the year 1505, and the equinoctial gales carried a nip in the air. But the sailing of the ships, already delayed several times, was now a certainty. There was a brisk impatience among the captains.

In one shadowy group beside a candle-lantern, several men and women clustered around a youth of less than twenty-four years. He was short and stocky, with black hair and gleaming black eyes. Particularly noticeable were his long, bushy eyebrows that set him apart from his shipmates. The memory of those bushy eyebrows lingered even after one turned away from him. His Portuguese name was Fernão de Magalhães, and he was destined to become a great master mariner and a world explorer. This was his first deep-water voyage.

A soft, kind voice was saying, "Fernão, my Son, remember your vows. Keep your cross close to your heart."

There was a far-off gleam in Fernão's dark eyes.

"Yes, Mother dear, I'll remember. Farewell."

"Hi there! You, young fellow! *All* ship's company aboard." A heavy hand shoved his shoulder. "Now up with you!"

"Aye, Sir. I'm going up, Sir."

The young seaman, gifts bulging under his arms, hurried up the gangway to his ship. Then slowly, under the quiet skies, could be heard the creakings of the blocks as the sails strained to the masts and, through the dark, the heavy breathing of the men hauling away on the lines. Gradually, the masts of the twenty-two vessels glided gently out into the slow-moving current. Pungent tidal odors filled the air as the dark hulls stirred the waters and drifted past the jagged towers of Belem, ghostly white against the darkness, and moved on.

Trumpets screamed eerie crescendos, and the drums beat their last, sad farewells from the fading quay. Mysteriously, silently now the fleet moved down the Tagus, then turned south at its mouth, and out onto the great sea, past Cape Saint Vincent to be swallowed in the rolling gusts of fog from the cold Atlantic.

Half around the world to the Spice Islands in the East they were destined to go. Down the black African Coast to double the formidable Cape of Good Hope with its gales, hail, and lashing rains. Thence out into the blistering heat of the Indian Ocean and on through scorching weeks across tropical seas to their final destination in unexplored waters.

Manning the fleet of twenty-two ships were fifteen hundred men. One of the ships bore the lad christened Fernão de Magalhães, later known to the world by his English name, Ferdinand Magellan. This lad was only a sobresaliente, or supernumerary, a youth without even the rating of able seaman. He was just one of the extras who pitched in to pull on the lines, scrub the deck, or to fight on shore or on shipboard as a common foot soldier. But he was expected, too, to give up his life for his country in a time of need.

Here, at last, was his dreamed-of opportunity. Great adventures lay before him. He breathed the damp sea air in long, brisk, delighted pulls. In its wet tang he found the lusty food for his soul that he hungered for. The rise and fall of the ship, and the whine of the gale through its rigging were happy stimulants to his whole being.

Since leaving his quiet little town of Sabrosa, in the Province of Traz-os-Montes where he was born, he had been fortunate in having entrance to the royal palace of his king and queen, for his family possessed a coat-of-arms and was of noble blood. In the palace he studied mathematics and navigation diligently. When he wasn't studying, he spent his time along the harbor, where he learned everything he could from the men of the sea.

He practiced often with his sword and his crossbow so that he would have experience which would make him more valuable for foreign expeditions, should an opportunity arise to join one. He wished to improve all his chances of being chosen. All men desiring to go to foreign lands were required to learn the manly art of self-defense. He knew book learning was necessary, too, but most of all he wished to be able to participate in actual adventures.

Ferdinand was not content to stay quietly at home and obtain his excitement secondhand from the mouths of other adventurers. He realized that he was living in a world of swift changes. Everyone was talking of Columbus's wonderful voyages to far-off Hispaniola in the West Indies and of Vespucci's explorations to the lands of New England.

Everywhere men were setting foot where no other white men had been, and looking upon strange lands for the first time. From these faraway places they were bringing home rich treasures and valuable knowledge. And as the achievements of one courageous man arouse courage in the hearts of all men, so had these great explorers fired ambition in Ferdinand Magellan. Although he loved the sleepy hills around his home at Sabrosa in Traz-os-Montes, and cherished his family deeply, his true love, his innermost burning flame was for adventure.

He even dreamed of possessing a ship of his own one day, and becoming an explorer himself. He could not believe, as did some explorers of his day, that the earth was flat, that vicious sea monsters could swallow a ship whole, or that in tropic latitudes the heat of the sun melted the pitch in the decks so fast that the planks separated and the ships fell apart.

These silly rumors infuriated the clear-thinking Magellan. They were myths, he believed, which were the deliberate fabrications of cowardly men who were afraid to explore beyond the coasts they already knew.

There was one thing of which Magellan felt very sure. If he could captain a ship himself, and sail it completely around the world, he could easily disprove all these myths. So far, of course, a circumnavigation of the world had never been attempted; in fact, it had not even been thought of. And, of course, no one had yet heard of the Pacific Ocean.

There was one person who believed in Magellan. This

was his cousin, Francisco Serrano, who was accompanying him on this voyage to the Orient. Together, they would pace the deck at night. While Francisco, who was a born romanticist, extolled the beauties of the heavens or the picturesque pattern of some constellation, the practical Magellan would instruct his relative on the changing angle of one of the stars and its effect on their compass. And despite the difference in their temperaments, the two passed many pleasant hours in each other's company.

But to Magellan his dream of possessing his own ship seemed so far from being realized that he often became frustrated and discouraged. At such times Francisco would give him the hope and encouragement he needed. And although he could not see how he was ever going to be able to attain his great ambition, Magellan never gave up thinking about it and planning for it. He knew that he must keep on studying and learning. And he always looked for ways whereby he could distinguish himself in his shipboard duties.

His ship would be his school. Her captain and his officers and sailors, whether they knew it or not, would be his teachers. He realized, too, that he was luckier than most young men to be "going to school" on a ship. He would not balk at the most miserable task assigned to him. In this way, when an opportunity for promotion arose, he would be ready to qualify for it.

He must learn all about the winds and storms, the ways of the ocean currents, and of that greatest of all bugaboos, longitude. Knowledge, he knew, removed fears. With knowledge, he was sure some day all men would be able to sail anywhere, unafraid.

In his hunger for learning, however, Magellan aroused the jealousy of his less ambitious mates. But he was courageous. He permitted nothing, absolutely nothing, to block his ambitions. He saw that many men were unfit for the lonely life at sea where there was nothing but the rolling decks below, the wide skies above, and the vast sea all around.

Some men became fidgety, or bad-tempered, or morose. The sea was too powerful for them. These men, he thought, should have stayed ashore and remained landlubbers.

2

The way of a ship

Magellan was never lonely at sea. He could walk for
hours studying the changing constellations, listening to
the whine of the sea wind through the rigging, and the
parting of the waves against the plunging bows. He
said that the sea talked to him, and thus he was never
without companionship during the long hours of the
night watches. In addition, his mind was too active for
him to have any patience with loneliness.

His chance to distinguish himself came sooner than he expected. King Manuel of Portugal was sending Captain-General Almeida to try for the first time to reach unknown lands in the Sunda Sea. The fleet was ordered to put in first at Mozambique on the East African Coast, then at Melinda, another port a hundred miles farther north. From there they were to sail for Cannanore in India; and thence to Cochin, India, on the Malabar Coast.

En route the vessels were to trade the wares they brought from Europe: scarlet cloth, olive oil, wines, sugar, clothing, and coral. In return they were to endeavor to bring home ivory and gems from Africa; and from India they were to bring cloves, cinnamon, ginger, peppercorns, and fine silks. In addition, the expedition was commissioned to "carry the Cross." This meant they were to spread Christianity to all unenlightened people along the trade routes.

Enormous religious crosses, made of wood and painted snow-white, were carpentered for the fleet. These were sometimes as tall as twenty feet. They were sent ashore to be raised on some conspicuously high ground; if possible, on the nearest hill. Under these great crosses the Captain-General and his commanders held religious services, instructing the natives to disa-

Raging storms lashed and battered the ships

vow their wooden idols, cannibalism, and murder, and
to live by the Golden Rule, loving their fellow man.
Most of the crusading captain evangelists were enor-
mously successful in winning over the savage peoples.

After a perilous voyage of three months during
which one of the ships leaked so badly that it had to be
abandoned, the fleet reached the stony heights of the
Cape of Good Hope. Once it had arrived at these forbidding cliffs, however, raging storms lashed, battered,
and scattered the ships for nearly two weeks. After the

storms had subsided, it was discovered that two men
had been washed overboard.

Relatively mild weather now set in, and soon the
ships were in the calm waters of the Indian Ocean.
Northeastward, off the African coast, lay a landlocked
bay, and here Captain-General Almeida rested his crews,
traded with the natives, and gathered a fresh supply of
green vegetables, provisions, and water. Preparations
were made for leaving. Final religious services were
held on shore for the crews and the natives.

The fleet then sailed for Kilwa, the most important
city on the East African coast, where the Captain-General had orders to set up a trading post. The Arabs resisted, but they were powerless against the Portuguese
invading force.

For the next two years Magellan was kept busy patrolling the Portuguese-held coast and helping his superiors with the conduct of civil affairs. Then he went
off on another voyage, this time to India, where once
more he had many adventures. In 1509 he took part in
a daring naval engagement in which the Portuguese
vanquished the Egyptians. Magellan himself was seriously wounded in this battle.

Upon his recovery there arose an opportunity to see
even more of the world, and Magellan eagerly grasped

it. Francisco de Almeida, now a Viceroy stationed at Cochin in India, was organizing an expedition to sail in search of the Spice Islands, or the place of spices, considered possibly to be a continent in the Sunda Sea in the Far East. Ferdinand Magellan and his cousin, Francisco Serrano, were among those chosen for this special expedition.

Owing to the unsettled military conditions along the Malabar coast, Almeida felt it unwise to lead the expedition himself. Portuguese interests were of vital importance and had to be protected. To the practical-minded Almeida, explorations for the vague Islands of Spice, or to the strange coasts of Cathay (old China) were less important than safe and adequate protection of already acquired Portuguese properties.

Accordingly, he outfitted Captain Diogo Lopes de Sequeira with five ships, men, and provisions and instructed him as to his mission. A brilliant navigator, Captain Sequeira had an outstanding record for finding his way in and out of strange and unknown places. His mission was to "spy out" the unexplored regions for a mainland, or the fabulous Islands of Spice. Along the route, he was to collect rare trade goods and set up Portuguese trading posts. He was also to carry on the crusade for Christianity.

The command of the ship on which Magellan sailed was given to Captain Garcia de Sousa. De Sousa was probably Almeida's most capable captain. He was the most kind and the most delightful of all the Viceroy's commanders. He was also known to be a sailor of great daring, and a man who attracted courageous men. Magellan considered himself fortunate to be serving aboard Captain De Sousa's ship, and was exultantly happy to be participating in this great exploration expedition.

When Sequeira's explorations were over, four of the ships including Magellan's were to report back to the Viceroy at Cochin for further orders. But Captain Sequeira in his flagship was to sail directly home to Portugal. He was to report his findings to King Manuel and to take with him a shipload of rare trade goods, it was hoped, from the Spice Islands.

The fleet departed. For several weeks they sailed westward across azure seas and through fine weather. Eventually they sighted a group of small islands, now believed to be the Nicobar Islands, about two hundred and fifty miles north of Sumatra. However, Captain Sequeira did not stop there. He was seeking larger islands or, he hoped, a great mainland. As the weather continued to hold fair and the fleet had a favorable wind, he felt he should continue probing for the greater prize. In the end the brave commander's resoluteness was rewarded. At dawn on September eleventh, 1509, a beautiful emerald peak rose out of the sea. By mid-afternoon the ships were off a broad coastline that faded off into limitless distances far north and far south.

Seeing no life along the strange coast, nor harbors, the wily commander sailed southward with his fleet all the remainder of the afternoon. He was certain that, at last, he had discovered the mainland of a great continent. And so he had. He was the first explorer from Europe to be cruising along the tongue of the Malay Peninsula, which is part of the vast Oriental land mass jutting out from Cathay (China) and Siam.

The tropical coast itself presented an idyllic scene. White surf in endless beauty rolled up wide, clean beaches fringed with green, swaying coconut palms. From the shore verdant forests rose everywhere. The trade winds were warm and soft, soothing and scented. The seas were calm. The skies were a brilliant blue.

The atmosphere was that of another world. To each sea-weary seaman on board the five ships, the day was one of memorable enchantment. And just before sundown the commander earned the real reward for his sustained patience and fortitude. Pinnacles of steeples studded with jewels and tall minarets gleamed from beyond the sultry beaches ahead. Columns of smoke rose from many chimneys among the green hills; and soon they beheld a thriving city. Then the coastline opened before them between two capes, revealing a fine, landlocked harbor. Breathless with astonishment, Commander Sequeira and his men stared, and sailed in.

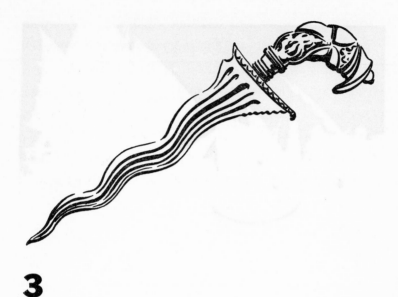

3

Lands of the Golden Dragon

The fleet had reached the other side of the world. They were at the great Orient trading center of Malacca. On board Captain De Sousa's ship, Ferdinand Magellan gazed unbelievably at the scene of beauty that stretched before him. He was more than twelve thousand miles from his Lisbon home. Yet here stood a city appearing more beautiful and even more civilized than the great European city of Lisbon from which he had just come!

At the great Orient trading center of Malacca

It was totally different from anything he had ever expected. Queer, twin boats called catamarans, with slanting lateen sails of woven fiber, darted swiftly under the sterns, while brown, friendly faces looked up at the sailors, fascinated. Beyond, in the harbor, were lumbering junks from China. And there were other strangely designed hulls, sleek, large, and heavily laden, making frothy wakes as they plied their courses.

It was a tranquil bay of small, tumbling whitecaps, bright sunshine, and happy laughter. The town was thickly settled, and for long distances up and down the coast many fine homes could be seen through the lush green foliage. Enormous mosques, white and clean,

loomed in the tropic sunshine. Most impressive of all,
was a massive fort that glowered over the city. It had
heavy stone bastions and thick mortar walls. This, too,
was a larger and a more powerful fortification than any
Magellan had ever seen in his native Portugal, or Spain,
or even India.

Malacca was obviously a trading center of enormous
wealth. Yet, while nothing had been seen of the inte-
rior of the city, there was outward evidence everywhere
that the explorers were face to face with a civilization
much older than their own. During his previous stays
on the Malabar coast Magellan had heard many wanderers' tales about this fabulous land of the Orient. But
this! This was beyond all belief!

Magellan was thrilled and enchanted. The lands of the
Golden Dragon! Here was adventure, rich and meaty.
It was for this that he had been waiting so long. Excitement rippled through the entire fleet. Every seaman
wanted to get ashore as quickly as possible in order to
view with his own eyes this colorful tropical Paradise.

The decision for granting leave rested with the flagship. But Captain Sequeira, although an expert mariner and a daring explorer, did not always analyze sit-
uations realistically. For example, he presumed that
because most people everywhere were friendly to the

Portuguese, the people in Malacca would be friendly too. He believed this in spite of the fact that he knew nothing about the Malaccans.

Having brought his armada into the unknown waters of Malacca Bay as expertly as if he were sailing into his own Lisbon, Captain Sequeira had no fear of the shore, nor of any adventure awaiting him there. His loyal seamen deserved leave, and he was not a man to deprive his hard-working men of their pleasures. He immediately granted liberty to the entire fleet. He also permitted all natives free access to his ships. So far he had no reason to believe that his squadron was not among friends.

But the Sultan Mohammed, who was ruler of this Gibraltar of the East, had heard alarming tales of the grasping powers of the Portuguese. Reports had been brought to him of the hard rule they maintained along the Malabar and the Madras coasts. He was filled with anxiety as he looked at the ugly black snouts of the Portuguese cannons pointing at his splendid city.

Too often had he listened to the wild stories related to him by the cameleers of the deserts, as they described how the Portuguese had maneuvered a stranglehold on all the caravan routes into India. Now, with the arrival of the Portuguese at his own distant gates, he was consumed with fear and foreboding. Here was a dangerous threat to his sovereignty. Such a menace, he felt, should be nipped in the bud.

Meanwhile, Ferdinand Magellan, true to his impetuous nature, was one of the first to set foot on this foreign coast. He, too, had to see with his own eyes, as quickly as possible, this fabulous shore. Accompanied by his cousin, he strolled up the main street, finding himself charmed by the musical bells and the flutes of the vendors, the exotic scents from the perfumed bazaars, and the throngs of gayly turbaned natives. Stopping beside a tiny fruit cart, he picked up a long yellow fruit. The eager peddler stripped back the golden peel and gave the fruit to Magellan. This was the first time any European had tasted the fruit that was later to become a world favorite—the banana.

However, after but a brief time on shore peering into winding alleys and exotic shops, Francisco Serrano's shrewd eyes detected that he and his shipmates were being surreptitiously trailed by some armed Malaccans. Trying not to show their suspicions, he and Magellan slipped away and sped back to their ship. There could be a danger here, they felt, for the entire fleet.

Serrano went directly to Captain De Sousa and, endeavoring to show as little concern as possible, whispered his fears to the Captain. De Sousa looked around him thoughtfully. As he stroked his chin whiskers Magellan could see that there was real concern in his expression.

De Sousa was quick to perceive their danger. The fleet was vastly outnumbered by the natives now swarming over the ships, and with the larger portion of their seamen and soldiers ashore, the Portuguese might easily be overpowered, captured, and every man-jack murdered. The sweat started to break out on De Sousa's brow. He realized that their plight might be a desperate one.

Placing complete trust in Magellan, De Sousa whispered several orders to him. First, a sentry was to be posted in the mizzen-top to report any unusual activity seen on the shore, or any armed parties approaching.

Next, Magellan was to row with all possible speed to the flagship to warn Commander Sequeira. Finally, he was to continue on to shore. There, he was to get word quietly to every seaman and soldier to return to his ship immediately. It was a large order. Too, it was rapidly growing dark, for in the tropics there is no twilight, just sunset. In one stride comes the darkness; then the stars burst forth.

Lights were already dotting the shore. But Captain De Sousa had chosen his emissary well. Nothing short of death would halt Magellan on this mission. Quickly he alerted the sentry, who hastened at once to his lookout station in the mizzen crosstrees. Then he quietly set off in a swift little gig, rowing furiously for the flagship.

Barely had he shoved off from the side of his own ship, however, when he heard the sentry's astonished outcry. This was the first warning of impending danger. Magellan rowed even more desperately. Would he be in time to avert disaster?

4

On a far foreign shore

Barely soon enough Magellan made fast his gig to Commander Sequeira's gangway. Barefooted, he raced noiselessly to the deck. In grave fear, he saw six huge Malays standing around his leader who was seated, chatting with several of the shore-side officials. All, Magellan noted, were heavily armed.

Reaching Sequeira's side, he leaned over and whispered the warning. At first the commander seemed reluctant to believe the astounding report. Then as his eyes strayed over the armed Malays scattered around the decks and the several well-armed natives beside him, the muscles of his bronzed face tightened. His dark eyes narrowed thoughtfully.

Suddenly a huge puff of smoke arose from the upper walls of the fortress. It was the signal to commence the attack for the capture of the Portuguese fleet! The big Malay standing behind Sequeira raised his kris over the commander's head. Sequeira, though, was too swift. He dropped forward to the deck and, as he leaped away to safety, he drew his sword and ran two of the Malays through the chests. They dropped to the deck, dead.

Magellan, now standing back to back with his commander, assisted in his desperate defense. Fortunately the flagship had a sufficient number of seamen on board to handle the situation. In a few minutes the bloody attempt was quelled. At this point all the Malays were either screaming for mercy or leaping overboard in a last frantic attempt to save their lives. Even so, the Portuguese killed many with their arquebuses and swords, either as they leaped or after they were in the water, struggling to swim away.

Obtaining additional seamen, Magellan again dropped into his gig and, with Sequeira's blessing,

The Malays were leaping overboard

raced for the shore to lend assistance to the men
trapped there by the enemy. Already the screams of the
Portuguese could be heard as they dashed for the beach
to their waiting boats. It was apparent to Magellan that
a full flight was in progress. But his shipmates on the
beach were so outnumbered that he held little hope for
their escape.

As Magellan drew nearer to shore, an icy chill swept
over him. He could see Francisco Serrano and several
seamen surrounded by many times their number of
Malay fighters. The Portuguese were putting up a des-

perate hand-to-hand fight, but losing every inch of the way. The situation looked hopeless.

In angry resentment, Magellan beached his boat and rushed to Serrano's side. He fought like a mad beast, slashing and stabbing at the Malays around them. In a few minutes, through a desperate rear-guard defense, and at great personal risk, he managed to rescue his cousin. The remaining Portuguese in the party were murderously cut down.

Thus, Ferdinand Magellan proved his courage as well as his loyalty. From that moment Francisco Serrano was, in truth, his blood brother. In later years, their staunch friendship was to prove invaluable to both men, but particularly to Magellan's success as a noted explorer and master mariner.

Amid the booming explosions of the Portuguese cannons, and the cannonballs crashing through the streets of the city, the Malays finally dispersed and ran for cover. None had seen cannons before. And, of course, none had heard their terrible explosions, nor seen the results of their frightening destruction. In terror, they quickly gave up the fight. Almost at once the streets had become completely empty and deserted.

On shore the Malays gathered here and there in groups to blame one another for the treachery against the Portuguese who had done them no harm. They were remorseful for their attack against the peaceful seamen. The Sultan, too, began to realize his grave blunder. He knew that the Portuguese would eventually exact reprisal. He had seen that they could fight like devils. In fact, he was quite sure that they would be an irresistible enemy.

Sultan Mohammed's mistake was that he didn't think of all of this soon enough. Now he sat on his luxurious throne in complete anxiety and confusion.

Commander Sequeira gathered his captains around him for a council. A truce messenger was dispatched to shore in the hope of ransoming some of the men. But the Malays failed to reply to the offer. Sequeira believed the reason was that none of the Portuguese remained alive, although he possessed no proof.

The next day, after the fleet had sailed, De Sousa's ship was attacked by Chinese pirates. It was at this moment that Magellan made himself the singular man of the hour. His chance to prove himself useful in a crisis had arrived, and he grasped it well. Leading the Portuguese in a furious counterattack, he slashed at the Chinese so effectively that they abandoned their ship with its cargo of valuable plunder. The captured ship, with a prize crew aboard, was towed alongside Sequeira's vessel.

All would have gone well if it had not been for a sudden storm that hurled the captured ship dangerously against the side of the flagship. Fearful of disaster, Sequeira gave orders to cut the towline. And once again Magellan proved himself the man of the hour. Denouncing such an act, which would have meant certain death for the men aboard the captured ship, he argued so vigorously that Sequeira was dissuaded from carrying out his decision.

After port had finally been made on the Malabar coast, Sequeira sailed back to Lisbon. The rest of the fleet set sail for Cochin. There, although they were unaware of it, changes had occurred. Dom Francisco de Almeida had been supplanted, and the new ruler was Governor Albuquerque.

The great Malaccan adventure brought Ferdinand Magellan extraordinary honors. His name was on the tongues of all the men in the fleet. Promotion would be his. He had drawn a step closer to his dream. The glowing flattery he received from Francisco Serrano delighted and comforted him. He could see bright days ahead.

The return voyage to Cochin was made without further incident. Brought before Governor Albuquerque by Captain De Sousa, Magellan was cited for his outstanding achievements and promoted to the rank of captain. He was then ordered to join the Portuguese naval expeditionary forces on shore.

While here, he participated in a disastrous voyage to the city of Calicut. This expedition was under the command of Governor Albuquerque, who had decided on a surprise attack. The natives, however, routed the Portuguese in the worst defeat they had suffered in the Orient, and both Magellan and Albuquerque were wounded in battle.

This must have been one of Magellan's darkest hours. Yet, though he could not have known it then, disappointments were in store that were to cause him more pain than any physical wound he suffered. His relations with Governor Albuquerque worsened after an occasion on which Magellan sharply disagreed with the Governor. Albuquerque was not a man to forget. He made known his displeasure with Magellan in the reports he sent back to Lisbon.

5

The risks of exploration

Absent from his native land for nearly six years, Ferdinand Magellan received the sad news that his mother and father had died, and that his brothers and sisters had scattered to unknown parts. News by ship traveled slowly, and how many years his kin had been dead and missing, he did not know. This was a blow to Magellan. But he realized that in his adventurous life it was almost impossible to keep in touch with his people.

What had given him comfort all these years away

from the home was the invaluable friendship of Francisco Serrano, never more appreciated than during the tedious period of Magellan's convalescence from his recent wound.

Then one day Serrano told Magellan of his plan to remain in India. Portugal now ruled this land that Serrano loved so well. He no longer wanted the hard struggle of the vigorous life in Europe. He wished to spend the remainder of his days quietly in the colorful lands of the Golden Dragon.

Here, he said, were costly steeds, leopards, and coco palm trees bending gracefully over beautiful beaches. Here, too, were white elephants swaying majestically through the narrow streets and kneeling before the Holy Father. (Eventually, Portugal did grant Serrano his dearest wish by giving him ambassadorial status as Captain-General of Sunda Island, of the Amboina Group. Here he lived a long and useful life which completely enchanted him.)

At this point Magellan took stock of his status. He was now an experienced navigator, fighter, gunner, and an expert sailor. He was thirty years of age, a mature man. He treasured in his heart a deep love for the East. But more than this, he nurtured a wondrous dream of an exploration for his king and his country.

His dreams and highest hopes however, were destined for a delay. His homeward-bound ship, heavily laden with trade goods from the Orient, struck the Pedro Reefs of the Laccadive Islands. Almost immediately she broke up. The situation of the shipwrecked men was desperate. The officers declared their right to take the lifeboats and return to Cochin, leaving the men behind. Then an angry dispute broke out between the officers and the men.

To save the situation, and to uphold the dignity of the ship's officers, Magellan agreed to forego his own right as an officer, and stay on with the men, *if* the departing officers would promise to send aid quickly. This they promised to do, and Magellan, now a popular officer because of his many heroic acts, was able to pacify the injured feelings of the men quickly.

When the rescue ship finally did arrive at the Laccadive Islands, Magellan and the other castaways were picked up. They were then returned to Cochin, safely. And at Cochin, for his latest gallantry to his shipmates, and for the splendid military example he set for the naval services as an officer, Magellan was cited for his highly honorable and humane acts.

This time he was promoted to the rank of fleet captain. For Ferdinand Magellan this was a day of glory.

A rescue ship picked up Magellan and his shipmates

He had at last attained a status which was respected not only for its title but for the background of experience it implied. He was another step closer to his cherished dream.

The months passed. Then Magellan participated unexpectedly in a most memorable voyage of reprisal to Malacca. This expedition was under the command of the ruthless and hot-headed Governor Albuquerque. He was doubtless chosen by the crown to teach the Malays a hard lesson in Portuguese strength.

The great fleet, consisting of nineteen strong ships

armed with heavy cannon, sailed into Malacca harbor at dawn and laid siege to Sultan Mohammed's stronghold. The revenging fleet pounded the city mercilessly, taking a terrible toll. Governor Albuquerque would send ashore a blistering barrage; then he would sail out. In a day, or perhaps two, he would return. No one knew whether it would be by day, or in the middle of the night.

Again he would hurl his awful instruments of death against the Malaccans. He maintained this suspenseful murder for six agonizing weeks, each attack timed with diabolical shrewdness to catch the terrified Malays off guard.

This frightening attack was exactly what the miserable Sultan Mohammed had long feared. The Portuguese had exacted a ten-for-one reprisal for their previous grievous losses. In the end, of course, Malacca was forced to surrender, and fell to the Portuguese. As the ferocious Portuguese closed their ranks during the last of the great battle and stormed the palace, the Sultan managed to elude his pursuers and fled the city on an elephant.

On searching the town, the Portuguese located some of their former shipmates from Commander Sequeira's voyage. They were still imprisoned, but alive.

Great was the joy of the released prisoners when they met their comrades again. The prisoners stated that they had been treated well while on shore. They came away with much valuable knowledge of life in this strange and distant world.

Again Magellan had distinguished himself as a bold and fearless fighter. As soon as the wounded Portuguese were attended and comforted, the fleet was organized, and set sail. When it finally arrived in Cochin, Magellan received orders to leave India for Portugal.

A strange feeling swept over Ferdinand Magellan as his ship plowed slowly up the Tagus River. He had left his home as an unknown. Now he had been halfway around the world. He knew that this was a great achievement, and that he had carved his name deeply on Portugal's historical tablets. He was a captain of the fleet.

In a way he was content. Yet he was impatient to go forward with greater plans. As his ship slipped slowly past the great white towers of Belem, he looked upon a different Portugal. His little church had been replaced by an imposing and grand cathedral. When he had sailed away seven years before, there was little shipping on the Tagus. Today the quays were clustered with hulls and sails, spars, and small boats. Docks and warehouses were piled high with cargoes.

From many sections of the waterfront could be heard the hammering of caulking irons and the building of large fleets. The port was gay with the multi-colored flags of all nations. Thousands of workers thronged Lisbon's narrow streets. There was an air of magnificence everywhere. Great ladies in rich finery rode past in gayly plumed carriages. Everywhere success and splendor were apparent.

Lisbon had become the first commercial capital of the world because of its vast trade with the East. He, Ferdinand Magellan, realized that he had played a part in bringing this thriving trade home to his people. For this he was glad. It was as if by magic that his homeland had become transformed into a new, and prosperous nation. And yet when Magellan, sunburned and bronzed, stepped onto his home soil, not a single friend or relation was there to welcome him. It was almost as if he was a stranger who had returned to some foreign land.

On shore there was talk everywhere about further explorations to the East. But for Magellan the East had been sufficiently explored. He wished to return some day, surely, to Malacca and the land of the Golden

Dragon. But now, he felt, the prestige of Portugal was ripe for a new glory. There should be an exploration to completely new parts.

And so it was that he gripped vigorously his dream for directing an exploration expedition himself—some voyage of fabulous worth. More than anything else, he believed, the world should be explored from Europe westward beyond Hispaniola and the Indies of the West. So far it was untraveled. What was *there?* This was the urgent question on many men's lips.

Thoughtfully he probed his plans. If there was a vast sea far off beyond Hispaniola, it could be crossed. If there was a great continent between, then this could be found. And at some place or another, he felt sure— through it or around it, north of it or south of it—there *must* be a new route and a better one, to the Malaccas. By this same route, he believed the Spice Islands could be found.

Success of his plans would include the first complete circumnavigation of the world. The glory of this discovery should be Portugal's. He was captain of the fleet. He was of noble blood. He could get an audience with his king. He would take his cherished dream to him at once. If only he could get ships! He clenched his fists desperately. If only he could! With this new hope born in his heart, he strode eagerly up Lisbon's narrow, cobbled streets toward the ancient Square of the Black Horse.

6

Magellan spins the globe

"Your Majesty," said Ferdinand Magellan, as he stood before King Manuel. "I come to you as captain of the fleet. I am now an experienced navigator, and I wish to offer my services to you and our country for an exploring expedition."

King Manuel drew his dark eyebrows together as he stared coldly at the weathered seaman before him. He had heard much of Magellan's fine achievements in the East. But Governor Albuquerque did not seem to think too highly of Magellan.

"An expedition—to what purpose?" asked the King, tersely.

"To discover for Portugal a shorter, new route, your Majesty, to the East. And at the same time to conquer rich new lands along the proposed route."

The King gripped the arms of his throne until his knuckles whitened. He appeared to be listening, and still he seemed not to hear. What was going on in the monarch's mind? It was as if he were listening inwardly to some foreboding spirit. Was he hearing some ancient grudge? Was it envy, or jealousy of the courageous man standing before him that made him tense? Magellan continued:

"I have studied maps drawn secretly by Prince Henry the Navigator and our own great cartographer, Ruy Faleiro. I am certain that I have knowledge of a new route, unknown to others, through the great continent to the west—the continent that stopped Christopher Columbus. After passing this continent I would hope to traverse the great South Sea. Then I shall surely find a more direct route to the East. Vast and rich lands must lie between. If your Majesty will but give me ships and men I will work earnestly in organizing such an expedition and——"

"I am not interested!" King Manuel blurted suddenly.

Magellan felt as if a hot rapier had been plunged between his shoulder blades. Had he heard aright? He knew that he had. He blanched. His shoulders sagged. This was hopeless disillusionment. He felt sick. His whole life's plan——

"Am I to understand," asked Magellan finally, in a voice so hoarse that he himself could scarcely hear it, "that my country has no further use for me?"

"That is the fact," retorted the King, bleakly.

"And does your Majesty then realize," declared Magellan with some heat, "that I shall be forced to offer my plan to other monarchs?"

"That is of no interest to me," replied King Manuel. "You may do as you please. Your audience is concluded."

Scarcely feeling his feet move across the great soft rugs in the royal room, Magellan, dazed and silent, left the palace halls. At a time when every maritime nation in the world was seeking a new route to India and Cathay, the King's decision was beyond belief. Every country hoped to avoid, in some way, the long, hard sea voyage around Africa, then the dreary overland caravan trek. The caravans were subject to every sort of peril, including sand storms, shortage of water, and vicious desert brigands. Why was his King so against him? It was a fact difficult to understand.

As for King Manuel, he had permitted one of the greatest and most adventurous projects that the world has ever known to slip stupidly through his fingers. His short-sightedness and stubborn refusal to endow the great Magellan with ships lost for him and his nation vast riches and untold glories.

Magellan's deep disappointment, however, did not discourage him. In fact, it seemed to sharpen his determination to get on with his cause. But as many men in great crises have turned with wounded hearts to the consolation of good friends, so Magellan sought out Ruy Faleiro, in Porto, for counsel and guidance.

Ruy Faleiro at this time was not only Portugal's greatest living astronomer and cartographer, but probably the most outstanding and wisest scholar in the world. In addition, he was a noted scientist in other fields, and a comforting philosopher. While he himself had never held a ship's trembling tiller, nor rowed through the waves with dipping oars, he possessed an unshakable faith in these practical abilities, and in the wondrous dreams of his friend and former school-fellow, Ferdinand Magellan.

Under a pale moon that night, sitting on a balcony overlooking a near-by river, these two friends came to a momentous decision: that each would renounce his citizenship to Portugal and go elsewhere with Magellan's great dream. That "elsewhere" they decided, would be Spain. During the evening Ruy Faleiro solaced his friend by saying:

"You must realize, Fernão, that the ambitions of our expedition are not for one nation alone, but for the benefit of all mankind. The all-important factor, therefore, is not whether any individual nation, such as Portugal, will underwrite it, but which one will have the foresight to do it. Let us make haste for Spain and see King Carlos."

It has often been asked, whether these two men shared a secret of a great strait through what is today the lower tip of South America. Yet even today no one knows the answer. It is an enigma buried in the past. But it is known that the two men smuggled into Spain what was even then a stained and ancient Schöner's Globe, and a secret chart made by a cartographer named Behaim. Did these contain their secret? No one really knows.

It is believed that not over a dozen Schöner's Globes existed in the world in Magellan's day. This globe was considered to be the most accurate spherical interpretation of the continents known at that time as well as the boundaries of the world.

The Behaim chart may have contained some valuable data on South America; data unobtainable from other charts or maps.

In any event, with the valuable information they possessed, Magellan and Faleiro were confident that they would succeed in discovering a new route to the Spice Islands. But they had to be extremely cautious in making their escape from Portugal. For, by the King's edict of November 13, 1504, it was a crime punishable by death to divulge information of unknown places unless authorized by the Crown to so do.

There were other obstacles too. In Magellan's day one of the greatest of these was a lack of information of any sort on longitude, or the measurement of distances east and west. The only method known for computing longitude at this time was a crude system known as lunars. The word lunar refers to the moon. This system consisted in plotting a position from the moon and coupling this with a position gained from the stars at the same time. But only a few scholarly men, including

Magellan and Faleiro, were acquainted with this method. Most seamen knew only that longitude was a vague measurement east and west.

The accurate determination of the position of a ship on the vast ocean, Ruy Faleiro and Magellan knew, was yet to be discovered. This was a method of measurement that must, in some way, become a known and dependable reckoning to men at sea. Ruy Faleiro, who was the greatest authority of his day on longitude, had already constructed his own rough system of tables, the first known to the world.

Another serious obstacle to safe navigation and the measurement of longitude as well as latitude, was the error now known to exist in the compass. Today this is termed "variation of the compass." For at distances far from the North Magnetic Pole, located in northwest Canada, the compass needle swings many points to the east or west of True North, depending on the part of the world in which you happen to be.

In those years it was thought that the North Pole and the North Magnetic Pole were the same. Actually, the North Magnetic Pole is located nearly a thousand miles distant from the North Pole.

In Ruy Faleiro Ferdinand Magellan had found an

invaluable counselor in the great adventure that lay ahead. Yet the exploration problems that confronted him were many, complex, and varied, as he was to discover.

7

The glory of Spain

Before leaving Portugal, the thoughtful Ruy Faleiro had dispatched a letter to his good friend, Juan de Aranda, in Seville, Spain, announcing their expected arrival. *Señor* Aranda was the head of a powerful and influential ship chandlery and ship-supply house known as India House. Further, he was in good standing with King Charles V, ruler of Spain.

The arrival of Ferdinand Magellan and Ruy Faleiro

in Seville seemed prophetic of better days right from the start. The very air, on that twentieth day of October, 1517, seemed electrified. It was scented with the sweet perfume of autumn leaves and the pungent odor of tar from the many ships on the nearby Guadalquivir River.

In this beautiful city fringing the dreamy river, there was an atmosphere of romance and adventure which prosaic Lisbon lacked. Music floated out on the crisp morning air from the cobbled side streets. Soft columns of charcoal smoke drifted skyward here and there. The jingle of burro bells, too, filled the air with tinkling merriment.

At first Magellan had been frightened by the prospect of leaving his homeland to start a completely new life in a new land. But almost at once he found himself falling in love with beautiful picturesque Spain, her great castles, and her happy, smiling people. Here, he felt, his own personality would find expression.

In Seville, the great cause of Magellan's arrival was substantially strengthened by the accompaniment of Ruy Faleiro who was well known to Spain as a scholar of unusual eminence. Magellan's practical seaman's experience welded with the sound learning of Faleiro was a perfect and impressive combination. Almost immediately an appointment was arranged by *Señor*

Aranda, and the two men presented themselves before a council from the wealthy India House.

This conference however, proved unfruitful. India House was a hard-bitten organization interested in but one factor—commercial profit. While they recognized definite possibilities in Magellan's proposals, to them everything seemed far too problematical and vague.

Juan Aranda, though, had been deeply moved by Magellan's pleas to his board, and he was convinced of Magellan's sincere convictions in his own dream. He was certain that Magellan had no will-o'-the-wisp castle-in-the-air, but something wonderful and lucrative. However, it would require a sponsor with genuine vision to recognize and evaluate it. The first man to see, Aranda felt, was Bishop Fonseca, Prince President of the Council of the Indies.

Forthwith, Aranda made contact with the Archbishop. He took with him, to aid in seeking an audience for Magellan, Ruy Faleiro. Magellan was a man, the two emissaries pleaded, who could do Spain a great service if his enterprise were supported. Here was a well-tried team, an experienced navigator and a noted cosmographer, impatient to throw all of their zeal into a sterling project for Spain alone.

The Archbishop, while showing great interest,

pointed out that the rudiments of any such plan had to
be weighed first by The Royal Council. So, offered the
Archbishop, this shall be arranged for you. Subsequently, Magellan did appear before this learned body.
And after an extremely long and difficult harangue, he
finally convinced these realistic businessmen that his
plan was reasonable and honest.

The men of the Royal Council were experts on mat-
ters of navigation and the troubles involved in defray-
ing the costs of a great expedition. This august body
had interviewed such great men as John Cabot and
Christopher Columbus. Too, they had seen Columbus
fail in his attempt to find a route to Cathay and the
East because he was stopped at Hispaniola by a great
land mass in the Western Indies. If Columbus had
failed, could Magellan succeed? After listening to him,
the Royal Council believed he might.

Favorable recommendations were sent forward to
the King. King Charles then agreed to an audience
with Magellan. Once in the presence of this monarch,
Magellan pleaded his cause well.

"Your Majesty," he declared with earnest convic-
tion, "there *is* a route beyond the Western Ocean,
and a great strait through that far southern land mass
between us and the East. Ruy Faleiro and I possess its

secret. We alone know where to find this pass. Equip me with a fleet and I will sail to the west and prove it to you by circumnavigating the earth."

King Charles was gripped with the drama unfolding before him. His eyes were burning with hope, and with new visions and new horizons for Spain. His face was radiant. Magellan's courage and confidence pleased him. Finally he exclaimed:

"My good Magellan, you have come at a most propitious time! You are truly the man of the hour. I believe that you are a wise man with daring, learning, and foresight. Yes, you are the man for whom the whole world has been waiting. The man whom Spain needs!" He motioned to the Royal Council members, saying:

"Let it be decreed. Give this man the ships he requires, the men to man them, and generous supplies for two years. And give him your support and your enthusiasm. I am depending on all of you to bring new glories to old Spain!"

Magellan's blood raced exultantly in his veins. His great dream! It was coming true! What he had failed to accomplish in more than ten years in his native Portugal was now coming to pass within a matter of days in enterprising Spain! God bless the King!

It was agreed then that the Cross would go with each

ship to spread the crusade of Christianity abroad to all
the world, so that as many unenlightened races as possible could come to know the blessings of religion. All
lands contacted would be acclaimed as new colonies
annexed in the name of Spain. And Spain would
sparkle with a new prestige.

In those years, the Pope had intervened between
Spain and Portugal to settle the differences over their
two spheres of operations. Thinking of the earth as
though it were an orange, he cut it in half. On May 4,
1493, he declared that Portugal should have one half,
and Spain the other half. He drew a line down the map
in the neighborhood of the Azores and the Cape Verde
Islands. All the lands already discovered and lying east
of this line, he stated, would be Portugal's, while all
the lands already discovered to the west would belong
to Spain. This papal decree was called the "Bull" of
1493. Later, however, this boundary became popularly
known as the "Line of Demarcation."

Subsequently it will be seen that most of the lands
found west of Europe fell under the ownership of Spain.
However, this papal edict did prevent a great deal of
friction between the two nations, and maintained a
pacific equilibrium between them through the years.
Could this edict have contributed to King Manuel's

lack of interest in a western expedition? It may have.

Contrariwise though, Portugal or any nation sending out an exploring expedition *after* the date of the
papal decree could claim any lands *first* stepped upon,
in the name of its flag and king. It was a confusing situation. When the news leaked out in Portugal that
Ferdinand Magellan had succeeded in obtaining ships
and funds with the blessing of the King of Spain, King
Manuel boiled with rage. Immediately he ordered the
coat-of-arms on the Magellan home in Sabrosa defaced,
and its shield torn down.

Further, he at once dispatched spies to the court of
Spain to report in detail on Magellan's activities. Next,
he made violent attempts to place every possible
obstacle in the path of Magellan's success. In this con-
nection Ruy Faleiro seemed to possess an almost mysterious ability to anticipate dangers in the path of Magellan, and to prevent them or, at least, lessen their
impact. He was continuously warning his friend of various impending perils.

King Manuel seemed to have sensed that Magellan
would succeed and that this victory would be a reflec-
tion on his lack of foresight and vision. Meanwhile, in
Spain, King Charles issued orders that the ships for the
expedition be assembled. This task was entrusted to

Juan de Aranda, who purchased five merchant ships in Cadiz and had them brought to Seville.

At the same time, Bishop Fonseca persuaded Magellan to appoint one Esteban Gomez as his chief pilot. Gomez had had his heart set on an expedition of his own but had failed to get royal approval. As a result, he was extremely jealous of the favor shown Magellan and became one of his bitterest enemies.

In due course the five able ships arrived in Seville. The *San Antonio,* one hundred and twenty tons, and a little less than a hundred feet in length, was the largest, but not the most maneuverable of the five. Next came the *Trinidad,* one hundred and ten tons, and about eighty feet; she was the most capable sailer. Then *Concepción,* of ninety tons. And lastly, two small vessels: the *Victoria,* eighty-five tons; and the smallest, the *Santiago,* seventy-five tons.

Early one morning in mid-October of 1518, Magellan viewed these sturdy ships for the first time. They were anchored in Seville harbor, glistening in the dreamy Andalusian sun. They were a sailor's ships, well made and hardy. Magellan's heart stirred within him. He visualized these vessels, *his* ships, swinging at their anchors before the golden domes of far Malacca, outrigger canoes skimming the waters beneath their sterns.

He saw his vessels, off there, beyond beyond, on the other side of Eternity!

But, there was still the unknown sea to cross. No man, as yet, had spanned that great South Sea, later to become known as the Pacific, although Vasco Nuñez Balboa had looked upon it from the Panama Isthmus of Darien on September 25, 1513.

Because of her sleek lines, and the salty rake-and-slant to her masts, Magellan chose the *Trinidad* as his flagship.

A seasoned sailor, he knew ships as few men did. He recognized the superior characteristics of the *Trinidad*, and later his judgment proved wise. For, although the *Trinidad* was not the largest of his ships, she repeatedly showed her prowess as the most able and the fastest of his fleet.

8

Betrayal and tragedy

As Magellan stood on the *Trinidad's* stern and gazed
forward, the morning breeze thrummed a low whine
through the rigging, and the waves broke gently along
her side. It was good, he felt, to be aboard a ship again,
and this one was his own! He turned aft and studied her
picturesque stern lantern decorated in red, yellow, and
gold.

That light! It was the light of his flagship. For two

years the fleet would follow it around the world! What a dream come true! But there were difficulties, too—horrible, unnecessary delays, and deliberate obstacles. King Manuel's spies were everywhere.

While Magellan was recruiting his crews, there were men who discouraged even good and courageous seamen with their lies. "The ships are unsafe; they are only drifters," they whispered. "The food will be bad. This Portuguese madman is going into dangerous seas unknown to any man. You will never see your families again! Why seek an early death?"

Then Magellan, confident and keen, would stride among the men saying, "Here is adventure for real seamen with red blood and not water in their veins. Men of courage! You who really want to see the world! Step forward. Here is the greatest chance in your lifetime—a chance to participate in making world history, to become great. Join the fleet. Set foot on strange, unknown ground, where no man has ever set foot before. Join the greatest adventure in the world!"

Then the more daring would step forward to be counted. The town criers beat drums and announced the Royal Proclamation: "For Service to the Islands of Spice. A pleasant voyage! Rich rewards. A royal armada, powerful and safe!"

And so the crews eventually arrived—Basques and Flemings, great hairy, tattooed sailors, bowlegged from rolling decks, stoop-shouldered, many with arms hanging like gorillas, but all with the look of the sea upon their weathered faces. And there were Negroes from Gibraltar, and Genoese and Greeks—all eager to seek fame and fortune.

Magellan knew sailors, and knew how to pick the seasoned ones. He soon sloughed off the culls and had his crews organized. The old sailors watched Magellan as he tested strains, while setting up on the tarry rigging, or cautioned inexperienced supernumeraries on going aloft. They recognized in him the sinews and bronzed cheeks of the true seaman. They respected him and felt secure in their confidence in him as their leader.

One evening while they were fitting out the ships, Magellan saw his men working vainly to stretch the foot of a sail along the main boom. It was several hands too short! His enemies had delivered sails of the wrong dimensions! Magellan swore a black oath. This meant re-ordering, delays, discouragement.

That night, Ruy Faleiro met him, as usual, at the foot of the *Trinidad's* gangway with a two-horse carriage. But this time Faleiro thrust a small pistol and an evil-looking stiletto into Magellan's hands. Faleiro's scholarly face was pale as he warned:

"Be on your guard this night, Fernão. There is a vicious plot by King Manuel's firebrands to assassinate you."

Magellan laughed aloud, unmindful of the danger.

"Good old Ruy!" he exclaimed warmly. "Always looking after the safety of his comrade. But you worry too much. I can take care of myself."

"You are preoccupied with other things. Someone must continuously keep you alert," Faleiro cautioned. "And this I can do."

In a few moments the two good friends were speeding off into the night, engaged in pleasant conversation. It was late, and the waterfront streets were shrouded in a dismal falling mist that blanketed them in heavy darkness.

Suddenly the horses gave snorts of panic. The carriage careened to a screeching, swerving halt. Muffled voices filled the air. Out of the night a band of ruffians appeared and grabbed the bridles of the horses. The heavy footfalls of the brigands could be heard all around, but the darkness obscured any sight of them.

The carriage was overturned. Magellan and Faleiro

were pitched across the wet cobbles. Magellan felt cruel hands tearing his clothes and searching for his throat. He lashed out with his stiletto. There were moans and cries of pain. Blood was flowing. Shouts of anger filled the night.

"Mata o homen grande! Kill the big one!"* came the savage growl.

"Policia! Police!" Faleiro's voice pierced the darkness.

Out of the side-streets lanterns moved dimly. The police arrived. And as mysteriously as they had appeared, the assassins melted into the night. Magellan had taken note of the fact that the oaths he heard were in Portuguese. The incident was a shocking one, and a violent physical struggle as well.

"Fernão! Fernão! Are you all right? Are you safe?" It was Ruy Faleiro, shouting in anxiety.

"Sí, sí, good friend! Thanks only to your foresight, and your strong stiletto," replied Magellan feelingly. "That *was* a close call though, *amigo."*

It was so easy to kill a man in those quiet, lonely streets, Magellan now realized. As the full impact of the cold-blooded designs of his enemies smote him, he became conscious of the danger he was in. Moreover,

A band of brigands attacked Magellan and Faleiro

he recognized the need to make haste with the plans of his expedition before some greater disaster fell. He would press for an early sailing.

The shock of the attack, and a severe skull wound coupled with the heavy strain of the expedition, proved tragic for Ruy Faleiro. At his home, before dawn, the eminent scholar suffered a physical and mental breakdown. He was taken to a hospital, and Magellan was never again to see his devoted and highly esteemed friend. This was a sad and agonizing blow to Magellan, for he deeply hoped to share his successes as well as his hardships, with his loyal companion. Bitterness for

King Manuel and his henchmen surged up within him. He wondered what move of desperation his vicious enemies might attempt next.

The following day a riot was fomented on the docks by his foes. From the decks of the *Trinidad* Magellan watched hundreds of the angry dock-mob forming. A Spaniard infused by King Manuel's clever spies stood atop a bollard, waving his arms wildly and haranguing the seamen.

"Magellan a great navigator? Bah!" he shouted. "He can't even tell you what route he is going to take, can he? Why? Well, I'll tell you why. He doesn't even know himself! Are you all too stupid to see it? He's nothing but a Portuguese fakir."

Magellan had, of course, kept his sailing route a guarded secret. He knew that there were men, both Portuguese and Spanish, who would go so far as to steal his precious maps for themselves, if they could. The leader of the mob next pointed to the flag flying from the highest mast-tip of the *Trinidad*. Now howling like a maniac he shouted:

"Look there! It's the *Portuguese* flag! And on a ship of the Spanish Royal Armada! What an insult to the Crown! And once at sea, this scurvy Portuguese will abandon you Spaniards! You'll see. Tear down that hated flag, I say! Tear it down! Let's go!" He beckoned with swinging arm to the mob.

The hysterical horde surged forward and started up the *Trinidad's* gangway, pushing one another off in order to be first. Magellan ordered them to stop. They rushed past, knocking him aside. There were even some women in the angry crowd. The police, however, rushed in.

After a scrambling brawl, in which one of the rioters was killed and many were injured, the mob was dispersed. The flag which was thought to be Portuguese had been hauled down, trampled upon, and torn to shreds. It was not Portuguese, but Magellan's own personal house flag. Magellan's flag bore his family coat-of-arms, and resembled only slightly the Portuguese national flag.

The next day Magellan was called before King Charles. Some individual, believed to be Captain Esteban Gomez, had reported to India House that Magellan was swindling money from expedition funds and shipping it back to Portugal. This, it was claimed, was really what had caused the riot! After a quiet conference with the King, Magellan, with his genuine honesty, cleared his case.

"I never at any time doubted your loyalty," declared King Charles. "I only wanted to hear your story in your own words. Now continue your preparations with my blessings. Try to ignore these vile whisperers and troublemakers."

A little sickened by his many setbacks, delays, and false accusations, Magellan returned to his ships to continue the fitting out. During these difficult times, however, King Charles never wavered in his devoted loyalty to Magellan. This was a heartening contribution to Magellan's success. He knew that he did not stand alone. And the tougher the going, the stronger his determination seemed to grow.

There was one enormous obstacle, however, that he always faced. He could never be sure whom he could trust. Nevertheless, in spite of continued heckling and interference, in a few months he had readied his fleet for sailing.

Meanwhile, King Manuel had sent an emissary to Magellan with a huge sum of money in the wild hope of being able to buy off the famous navigator. How little Manuel knew Ferdinand Magellan! Perhaps there was no man in the entire world at this moment to whom such an offer could have meant less. For all the things in the world that Magellan wanted, and had wanted for years, were now his.

King Manuel was outraged. Magellan's life was threatened twice. But it was not possible to frighten this man in any way. Such attempts only sharpened his caution and his desire for revenge, and increased his hatred for his enemies. Such dishonorable methods, he was confident, never won success for any man. He was determined to carry out his plans.

Next, a desperate attempt was made to burn Magellan's ships. Fires were simultaneously set in three ships. One of the fires in the *San Antonio* turned the powder room into a raging furnace, but the flames were extinguished by fast action. The daring crew fought the fire, although they were all in grave danger of being blown up.

By now King Charles had become thoroughly incensed by these troublemakers. He resented the time wasted, and the fierce struggle Magellan had to endure at the hands of these ruthless villains. He commenced throwing suspects into jail with great abandon. Following a third assault against Magellan's life—this time in broad daylight on the docks—King Charles became anxious for the safety of his great navigator. He ordered that watchful guard be maintained over Magellan night and day, no matter where he happened to be. All suspicious persons seen lurking anywhere near him were instantly placed under surveillance. The ardor of the troublemakers soon diminished.

9

Castles in Spain

In the midst of all the terror and struggles Magellan had to endure in Seville, he managed to meet and to marry a fine woman, Dona Beatriz Barbosa. This loyal Spanish lady counseled and comforted Magellan, and contributed the wealth and influence of her well-known family to the cause of his great expedition.

It was in the summer of 1519 that Magellan con-

fided to the Spanish King the good news that his fleet
was in readiness to sail. Whereupon the King immediately issued the order for an official sailing date. He
also decreed: "Each and all on this voyage shall follow
only the opinions and the determinations of the said
Ferdinand Magellan."

As dawn broke over the fleet on Monday, August 10,
1519, all Seville was up and eager to view the historic
departure. Not all of King Manuel's spies, nor all the
malicious enemies sneaking around Magellan, had prevented his sailing. Magellan had an exultant gleam in
his eyes that morning.

Happily he glanced over his fleet. The hull of each
ship was painted a rich yellow. Around the hulls just
below the bulwarks ran a shiny black arrow from stern
to prow. The figurehead at the bow of each ship was
resplendent in gold. The sterncastles too, were gold,
bordered with Spanish royal blue. The masts were all
scraped down to their natural wood and glistened with
fresh oilings.

The rigging, deadeyes, and ratlines were tarred glossy
black, while the mast-tops were different on each ship.
The *Trinidad's* was flame-red, while the *Victoria's*
was bright orange. Thus it was possible to identify each

vessel easily. All the sails were pale yellow and, imprinted in brilliant scarlet on the mainsail of each ship, shone the great Cross of St. James.

As Magellan now viewed his fleet, impatient to sail, a warm glow of contentment and satisfaction filled his being. There was a swift yet efficient inspection of each ship by the Captain-General. He consulted personally with Esteban Gomez whom he had honored with an assignment as pilot of the *Trinidad*. On the *San Antonia* was Captain Juan de Cartagena, second in command of the fleet in the event of Magellan's sickness or death. Cartagena was proud to have the largest ship.

Next, Magellan had a few brief words about their route with Captain Gaspar de Quesada, of the *Concepción*, and Juan Sebastian del Cano, his pilot. Captain Luiz de Mendoza commanded the *Victoria*. The tiny *Santiago* was captained by Juan Serrano, who was none other than the older brother of Magellan's old friend, Francisco de Serrano, of the memorable Malaccan days.

Supplies were carefully checked, because once at sea there could be no returning, nor sending back for needed items. Sixteen extra compasses were delivered at the last moment. Magellan's fine planisphere, completely refurbished and in its leather case, was brought aboard.

The planisphere was a rough star finder. It consisted of a projection of the stars on a chart, or what is known simply as a star chart today. Placed on top of this was an overlay map of the world which revolved around the North Pole. By rotating this overlay map, a star could be located in the heavens. Its position was determined in accordance with the time of night, the location of the ship, and the season of the year.

Next to be brought aboard was the beautiful, specially gilded compass, in a majestically carved teakwood case which was to be Magellan's farewell gift to the King.

A tall, dark, and scholarly-looking individual appeared suddenly before Magellan and handed him a scroll from the King. It read, "Would the Captain-General be so good as to accept this fine person, Antonio Pigafetta, as his official chronicler to keep a careful documentation of all the happenings throughout the great voyage?"

Yes, he would, most certainly. Magellan had heard only good things of the most noted journalist in Spain. He would be most happy to have him.

"Thank you, Sir." Pigafetta bowed courteously. "I thank you so much for this marvelous chance. All my life I have yearned to witness some of the magnificent and dread wonders of the limitless oceans."

But now the royal paymaster was signaling the Captain-General from the dock. The men and officers were to be assembled at once along the ancient quay side; two hundred sixty-seven in all. Here each would receive an advance of four months' pay for his family. During the ensuing few minutes Magellan sat on the quarterdeck of the *Trinidad* and, with the aid of the royal counselor, made his will. So much could happen on this long voyage.

"On the day of my burial," he wrote with fast-moving quill, "three destitute men shall be clothed; and to each of them give a cloak of gray stuff, a cap, a shirt, and a pair of shoes, that each may pray to God for my soul. Signed: FERDINAND MAGELLAN, Commander of His Majesty's Royal Navies, and Captain-General of the Armada bound for the Islands of Spice."

A long, sad blast from the trumpets then called all the ships' companies to final religious services. The men were quickly lining up now. Then, slowly, the procession moved off—two hundred sixty-seven men, wending their thoughtful way toward the little chapel of *Nuestra Señora de la Barrameda.*

From the narrow, cobbled streets floated the singing of sweet voices and the clicking of castanets, and from doorways the tinkling of glasses raised in heart-warming toasts for the departing ones.

Lips were parted in affectionate smiles, and tears gleamed frankly on sad Andalusian cheeks. No one there was free from emotion. Heaving breasts struggled with outbursts, and throats were tight. These fine, bronzed men marching, marching, marching . . . departing for far off into that vague, darkened mystery of the unknown seas. And, *quien sabe,* who knows, to what unnamed terrors! "God save them! God bless them! Their ships so small, and His ocean so vast!"

The average age of the men behind the mast was twenty-three years. Those at the chapel knelt while the priest committed their souls and their brave venture to the arms of the Holy Spirit. Then there was quiet. Just the soft, gentle winds from the harbor, and the faint mutterings of those at prayer. . . .

Finally, the doors opened. Back to the ships now. The crowds commenced to cheer. Many were weeping for their loved ones; others crossed themselves. Wives,

All Seville was up and eager to view

mothers, sweethearts, brothers, sisters—when would they see these loved ones again? "God have mercy on these brave men!"

Now, from the quay, the men marched up the gangways to their ships. The Captain-General of the armada gave the order to cast off. Again the trumpets blared. Sails were spread to catch the morning breeze. The ships were cast clear. Now from the port came the thunderous

the historic departure of the five ships

booming of cannon. The people moved about, lining
the shore, cheering in deafening crescendos.

Ferdinand Magellan, standing proudly on his quarterdeck, feet spread far apart, looked aloft to his sails.
He was gayly bedecked in a gorgeous, gold-brocaded
Cape of St. James which was flung jauntily across his
shoulders. A light breeze lifted it, revealing its scarlet
borders. At that moment he was the greatest hero in

the world. The blood pounded through his veins with an exultant throb. His cherished dream was being fulfilled. Would the world ever again be quite so wonderful, quite so important? "Praise be to God on High! God bless the King!" Magellan murmured these praises fervently. Then aloud, he shouted:

"The flag! The flag!"

And then pennons, banners, and ensigns rose to the mast-tops. Yes! There it was! The Royal Standard of Old Spain, gleaming orange-and-gold against the bright morning sun. And then the fleet moved silently into the mysteries of the vast ocean.

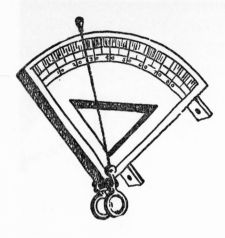

10

The open sea

The first landfall for the fleet was to be Teneriffe, in the Spanish Canary Islands, some seven hundred miles down the coast. That first night was a memorable one. The old seamen were getting back their feeling for the sea—their "sea legs." Youngsters, temporarily homesick, seasick, and barefoot, sloshed water down the decks, for the planks must be kept moist and tight and not allowed to dry out in the warm days ahead.

The silent stars, luminous and twinkling, seemed a bright prophecy for better days to come. The huge ship's compasses were lighted, while the lubber lines swung gently with the ship's motion, showing the course. Weathered quartermasters leaned jauntily on the huge oaken tillers and appeared like gods to the boys.

The ship's great hourglasses had been started at noon and were now swinging in their racks, the sand pouring relentlessly through them. From astern, beyond the *Trinidad's* foaming wake, came the echoes of bells, struck in pairs, sending magical messages to the ships that followed close behind.

Everyone seemed to be glad that the great voyage had at last commenced, especially the old seamen who were used to the rolling waves beneath them. Down in the cabin Magellan spread his great *portolanos,* or navigating charts, out before him and studied the courses to be run. Then he went on deck with his Behaim astrolabe of wood.

The astrolabe was a sixteenth-century instrument which crudely measured the altitude of sun, moon, or a star. It consisted of a circular piece of wood about a foot in diameter, containing graduations from o to 360 degrees around its rim. Fitted into its center was a movable indicator-arrow.

By holding the astrolabe in the hands and aiming its zero point toward the North Pole, then moving the indicator at the star desired, the star's angle from the Pole could be obtained. Also its apparent altitude in degrees above the horizon could be estimated.

The astrolabe gave only approximate results, its efficiency depending entirely on the expertness of its manipulator. From the data obtained, however, the approximate position of the ship was estimated.

The astrolabe was later replaced by the wooden, then later, the metal octant measuring from o to 45 degrees. The octant was then replaced by the quadrant measuring angles up to 90 degrees, and finally superseded by the excellent instrument in use today, the metal sextant, using a modern high-powered telescope which gives clear and delicately measured altitudes from o to 120 degrees.

Sitting at the foot of his mainmast, Magellan took an astronomical sight of the polestar, the first observation of the voyage. Antonio Pigafetta watched, enchanted, and later, below decks, he auspiciously commenced the journal which he so conscientiously maintained during the long months ahead.

The signal lanterns from the other ships were bobbing up and down on the dark sea, while from the stern of the flagship flared the Captain-General's signal: a huge torch of burning wood. This was fed continuously by the boys and kept burning throughout the night. For Magellan had willed that he should at all times keep the lead, and that the other ships should follow.

The men were chosen by their officers for the watches. They would stand four hours on duty and eight hours off, but the captains, pilots, navigators, and assistant navigators would stand four hours on and four hours off. And so that first night the ships settled into their routines, while the old sailors, behind sheltered bulkheads and out of the wind, talked of the fabulous treasures and beautiful maids waiting just for them in those far-off, fragrant Isles of Spice.

The night passed and morning broke with a sunrise of gold and scarlet. The officers were all on deck for the *diane*, or the watch for the morning star. The hulls and sails of the other ships of the fleet were now growing visible, their lights slowly fading with the dawn.

The telescope had not yet been invented, but old sailors with eagle-like eyes and extraordinary vision identified the other vessels. Far astern was the little *Santiago,* under Captain Serrano. She was pressing on all sail in her struggle to keep up with the larger ships of the fleet.

Magellan studied the smaller vessel and saw that with the increasing wind she was making hard weather of it. He ordered a thin red pennant hoisted to the main truck of the *Trinidad,* his prearranged signal for the larger ships to shorten sail. Topsails on all the larger vessels were then immediately doused in a seamanlike manner. The Captain-General saw this, and was pleased.

Thus the voyage continued. Magellan with Pigafetta and his navigators sat down on the main deck for their breakfast of mead (pale wine) and porridge. Coffee had not yet been discovered by the Europeans. And Magellan, sitting, sipping his wine, watching a school of dolphins cavorting near by, knew that he would never become indifferent to the magic and the wonders of the sea.

On the seventh day the fleet arrived at the beautiful little port of Santa Cruz, on Teneriffe Island. Here, for about fourteen days, the men rested and became acquainted with their ships. Fresh water and firewood

The swift little caravel bore a message for Magellan

were stored on board. A small cargo of pitch for trading purposes was loaded, as well as fresh vegetables, also, some live cows, goats, and pigs for slaughtering on the long voyage.

Just before sailing, a small craft, a swift little caravel of lateen rig, came speeding into port. She flew the flag of Old Castile, Spain. A boat from the *Trinidad* was sent to her at once. It returned with special dispatches from India House, together with an astounding letter from Diego Barbosa, Magellan's father-in-law. It read:

Capitan-General Mio:

Be of great caution. Captains Gomez and Cartagena are said to plot a mutiny, and plan to take your life, then to take over the fleet.

They have told their families here that should you give obstacle they will surely kill you.

We pray for your safety, and urge you to take every possible precaution.

We all send you our affectionate good wishes for your well-being.

DIEGO BARBOSA.

Magellan crumpled the letter containing this horrible news in his fist. Heaving a deep sigh, he brought his hands down hard on the gunwales of the *Trinidad* and stared out across the distant sea. Gomez, to whom he had been so kind! And Cartagena, who came so highly recommended by Bishop Fonseca! Were treason and treachery to follow him even across the lonely waters of the vast ocean? Were his officers not to be trusted? Where was the integrity of his fellow man?

11

Troubled horizons

On the third of October, the fleet sailed from Teneriffe. First down along the African Coast, then seaward across the long miles to the south and to the west. From the very start they were faced with dirty weather—day after day of flying spume, great mountainous seas, and the never-ending din of gales shrieking through the taut rigging. The little vessels reeled and plunged wearily through the wallowing seas, struggling against storms of unbelievable fury.

Then one black night a strange specter was seen—one seldom viewed at sea. St. Elmo's Fire appeared in a ball of brilliant flame on the *Trinidad's* mast-top. The mysterious fire lighted up the decks and the men's tired faces. Was this a holy sign? If so, what did it portend?

But the Captain-General's heart gladdened. Surely this marked the breakup of the foul weather. The following pre-dawn hours brought a deluge of rain. Shortly after, the skies parted, showing the stars clear and crisp. Then dawn broke in a warm and beautiful sunrise. The heavy seas were already flattening. By breakfast time, trade winds had sprung up, fresh and steady, speeding the fleet favorably along its route.

Magellan signaled to all the ships their new course for the day. South by west it was to be. One of his ships, the *San Antonio* under Cartagena, pressed on sail and, drawing alongside the flagship, hailed it. A quartermaster on the *San Antonio* then asked Magellan:

"Why do you change course? Our 'captain-general' demands to know."

This was insolence. The first inkling of trouble. First,

it was basic courtesy that only the captains should speak in person to Magellan. Second, there was only one captain-general, and this, of course, was Magellan. Bristling with rage, the Captain-General shouted back:

"Follow your flagship and ask no questions."

Later in the day when the wind altered and Magellan was again forced to change course, he was close enough to the *San Antonio* to speak the course. Accordingly he called out Captain Cartagena's name, expecting to receive the correct answering salute.

"When you address me properly as 'captain-general,'" Cartagena barked back impudently, "I will answer you."

One of Cartagena's quartermasters then haughtily asked that the course be repeated. Magellan called out that he would speak only with Captain Cartagena, who in turn replied:

"I had the best man in my ship answer you. Next time I will speak only through one of my pages."

This was too much insolence for even the patient Magellan. He immediately issued orders for all the captains of the fleet to report aboard the flagship without delay. As his captains came on board and gathered around Magellan they noticed that he was armed and that his face was taut. As Cartagena stepped onto

Magellan had Cartagena manacled and led away

his quarterdeck, Magellan grabbed him by the scruff of his collar. Swinging him around face to face, eyes fiery, he demanded:

"What is wrong with you anyway, insolent one?"

"You stay too far to the east of the Line of Demarcation," Cartagena countered in a bald lie. "You persist in remaining within Portuguese waters."

"My course has no bearing on any Line of Demarcation," snapped Magellan. Then he flung the white-faced Cartagena from him saying, "From now on, you are my prisoner." To his men he shouted, "Put him in chains."

Cartagena was manacled and led away. The men could see plainly now that Magellan was not a man to trifle with. They knew, too, that the King had invoked in Magellan the power of the noose and the sword, full authority to execute, should the need arise. The captains, sobered, returned to their ships. Cartagena, in irons, was sent aboard the *Victoria* and placed under the charge of Luiz Mendoza. This proved unwise, for it developed that it was placing plotter Number One with plotter Number Two.

On the evening of November twenty-ninth, the lookout leaned down from the crows'-nest on the *Trinidad* to shout:

"Ahoy on deck! Land ho! Dead ahead!"

In the hazy distance rose the purple heights of a long land mass. It proved to be Cape St. Augustine on the central Brazilian coast, near what is now Pernambuco. Magellan, however, seemed to know that his strait was farther south. He made no attempt to land here, but continued southward down the coast.

The fleet, averaging about three and a half knots an hour, or eighty-five to ninety miles a day, proceeded to what is now Rio de Janeiro. They arrived there on December thirteenth, and came to anchor in the port. A previous attempt had already been made to establish an early trading station here. Both Solis and Pinzon had traded in Rio in 1497, and again in 1508.

The crews, restive and bored after their long voyage, were happy to see the shore once more. But something else, Magellan noted, was creeping into their ranks. This was an undercurrent of arrogance and brooding. Somewhere, someone was kindling dangerous fires of hatred and rebellion against him. Meanwhile Pigafetta the chronicler was honestly recording in his journal the happenings of the voyage.

Of the Brazilians he wrote that the people went about completely naked and that their heads were shaven. When captives were taken in battle from enemy tribes, they were eaten. This was done, he said, solely for revenge and not because they liked or needed the meat.

The Spaniards, the Brazilians said, had come down from heaven. And as the native people had never seen ships as large as the Spanish ones, they said the great ships had spirits and were alive. The small boats, they

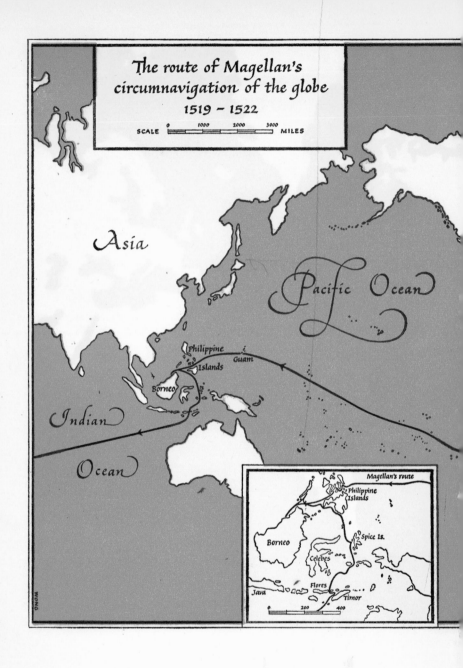

The route of Magellan's
circumnavigation of the globe
1519 – 1522

SCALE 0 1000 2000 3000 MILES

Asia

Pacific Ocean

Philippine
Islands

Guam

Borneo

Indian

Ocean

Magellan's route

Philippine
Islands

Borneo

Spice Is.

Celebes

Java

Flores

Timor

200 400

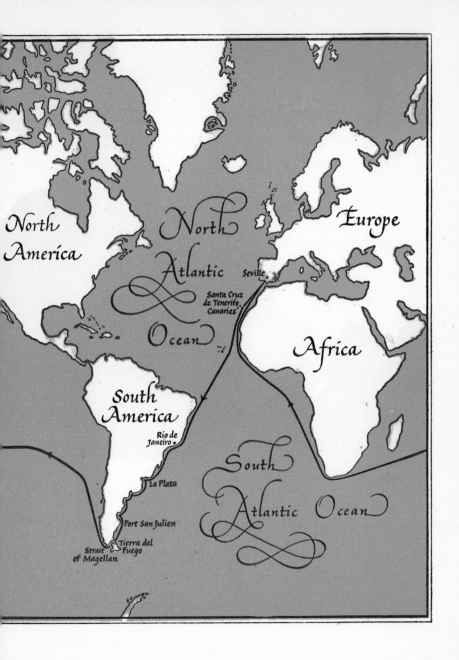

said, were the offspring of the mother ships, and when many of the small boats were resting alongside the mother ships, they pointed and said, "Look you! The mother ship now nurses her young!"

The natives here, continued Pigafetta, made canoes with stone tools and ate with similar ones. The men were well built and made fine oarsmen. Many lived to be one hundred and twenty to one hundred and forty years of age. They were very amiable and friendly to the Spaniards. The climate was tropical and the people of an easygoing nature.

But Magellan must hurry. Time was moving on relentlessly. There were thousands on thousands of miles to be put behind, and unknown lands yet to be reached. So, after a fortnight, refreshed and watered, with the ships freshly stored with tropical fruits and vegetables, they sailed from Rio de Janeiro.

As they journeyed southward along the coast, the land became more bold and barren, and the climate colder. The people on the far shore seemed more vigorous and less easygoing. They were clothed in warm animal skins. The winds blew stronger. Great combers, boiling white, towered high over the reeling bulwarks.

When the mouth of the great River La Plata spread before them, Magellan sailed in. He wished while here to settle one matter. Several explorers had announced that this surely was the entrance to the strait leading to the South Sea and the Spice Islands. Magellan was determined to find out if this was so.

Sailing several score miles up the wide river, the wily Magellan took continuous samples of the water. The current of the great river carried the brown waters slowly past the ships, always toward the sea which was now at their backs. When the buckets were hauled aboard, they were all found to contain *fresh* water. Not a taint of salt water could be detected.

This proved to Magellan that the water was not coming through any unseen strait from the salt South Seas. There was no ocean in that direction. Satisfied, he made a record in the journal and, heading his ships around, put to sea again.

12

On a lonely shore

Sailing close to the coast, Magellan drove south. The days wore on. The cold increased. The winds grew in violence. Great sea wolves and walruses appeared—animals unknown to the seamen. Odd-shaped birds hovered above the mast-heads. Strange new stars rose nightly in the heavens, and one constellation especially appeared as an omen. This was shaped in the exact form of a great Holy Cross, sparkling and shimmering against the cold vault of the night. Magellan gave it the name of the Southern Cross.

From the shore, savage wind squalls rushed at them, straining sails and rigging to the utmost. Strange scents of perfumed grasses and sage came downwind off the far shore, smiting the seamen's nostrils and intriguing their imaginations. The coastline became treeless and boldly rocky. It was fringed white with frothing breakers and forbidding stone cliffs. On the ships the helms had to be double-manned, while more and more often sails split and halyards snapped like pistol shots.

As the vessels pitched and groaned under the terrible strains, the Captain-General realized that they must reach a haven soon in order to repair weather damages on all the ships. Searching the unknown coast, he found an opening and sailed in. The ships tore around the cold, bleak capes and, with bulwarks buried in flying foam, came to anchor in the cold, clear waters. Magellan named this bay Port San Julien (in what is known today as Patagonia) in honor of the saint of that day.

The winds howled, while overhead strange birds wheeled, looking down at the ships curiously. Life here was comfortless and desolate. The skies were a forbidding gray, so darkened with flying black clouds that the day seemed like night. Cold draughts penetrated every nook and shelter in the ships.

Six months had already gone by, and the course was barely started. Many of the men were discouraged and were beginning to be afraid that they would never again see their homelands or their families. Superstitions and gossip were prevalent. The Isles of Spice had now become a joke among many. Secret rumors were going around that there were better days soon to come and that they all might even soon return to Spain. But, hush! If this should happen, it would have to be under a different commander from their Captain-General! Perhaps, *quien sabe,* it might be Cartagena, or even Gomez. Time would tell. Meanwhile all were suffering with the extreme cold.

Magellan was not without knowledge of this ugly gossip. He arranged for a Mass at once. The cross was taken ashore. There, with the aid of his priests, he exhorted his men to have courage, to be patient, and for all to stand together for their king and the great victory ahead.

But by this time the rebellion was well organized. Some men unhappily declared that the Captain-General, in order to make good his impossible claims, could not now return to Spain unless he found the strait that he had bragged about. And that if he never found it, he would *never* dare return before the King.

All this searching along the coast, they said, and a half year gone by, and they had found nothing. How much longer would they be forced to bear this loneliness? A fortnight passed. Then one night, while the cold winds whined through the rigging, a strange sound was heard aboard the *San Antonio*. Captain Mezquita, loyal to Magellan, captained this vessel. These sounds, surely, were footfalls coming up his gangway. But in the middle of the night? Curious, Captain Mezquita dropped out of his bunk, slid into his slippers, and proceeded up the hatch.

Meanwhile on deck, Navigator Juan de Lloriaga who had the night watch, had been surprised by a band of mutineers. Stabbed in the back, he was overpowered and pressed against the bulwarks. He cried out:

"In the name of God and the King, what is this, mutiny? In Heaven's name go back to your ships, or you will all be executed!"

Quesada, one of the mutineers, whirled on him. "This man will undo all our work by his infernal yelling," he growled angrily. He plunged a knife into the navigator while a co-conspirator, Juan Sebastian del Cano, stood watch.

Navigator Juan de Lloriaga was overpowered by mutineers

With a low moan, the faithful Lloriaga slumped to the deck, mortally wounded. Just then Captain Mezquita, who had stumbled onto the scene, came face to face with the released prisoner, Captain Cartagena. For a second, astonishment numbed him. Before Mezquita had time to grab his weapons or summon help, the mutineers whipped their bloody swords upon him. Shoving him roughly to the rail, they held him prisoner.

At this point some thirty additional ruffians poured up the gangway.

"You'll hang for this!" warned Mezquita.

"Hold your tongue, or I'll kill you," snarled Quesada.

The *San Antonio* was now taken over by Quesada, and Cartagena took command of the *Concepción*. By this time the *Victoria,* under the command of the traitorous Captain Mendoza, was also in possession of the mutineers, whose next step was to move the three ships and anchor them across the mouth of the harbor to bar escape by Magellan with his two remaining ships. Mutiny was winning!

Magellan, his bronzed cheeks paling, clenched his fists. This was the crisis his father-in-law had predicted in the warning note he had received at the Canaries. He realized the danger of his plight. He had not, however, become a veteran of so many bloody fights in his life, nor the hero of so many battles, without gaining considerable experience in dealing with blackguards. Nor did the knowledge that the odds were overwhelmingly against him throw any fear into this tough fighting man.

But what was he to do? Any action, he knew, would have to be fast and decisive to succeed. Pacing up and down his quarterdeck for a few anguished moments, he was absorbed in thought. Meanwhile, the ribald jeers from the crews of the other ships floated across the gray waters. There were many men even on his own ship, he knew, who wanted to give up, join the mutineers, and return to Spain. But this Knight of St. James, Knight of Santiago, and Captain-General for the King of Spain, was not a man to violate his sacred vows to others, nor to quit at any stage of the game.

Magellan made his decision. The least clever of the plotters of the revolt, he figured, was Captain Mendoza, of the *Victoria*. He would work on him first. He then sent two trusted men, Espinosa and Barbosa, on a "truce" mission to the *Victoria*. Espinosa was to board and deliver a note. Barbosa, accompanied by a dozen good men, secretly armed, was to wait under the *Victoria's* stern. Espinosa boarded and delivered the note. It read:

> *Captain Luis de Mendoza:*
>
> You will report at once to
> the flagship.
>
> > FERDINAND MAGELLAN
> > Captain-General of
> > His Majesty's Armada

"Ho!" declared traitor Mendoza, with a sly chuckle. "I do not fall into any such trap!"

Mendoza, reading the document, stood near the rail. In an instant Espinosa stabbed him in the throat, killing him. Quickly Barbosa and his men, weapons in hand, charged up the gangway in a surprise attack. Tumultuous uproar and confusion gripped the *Victoria*. In the next few moments the vessel was forced to surrender, and soon was under way, headed for a position alongside Magellan's ship.

Quesada, on the *San Antonio,* was completely unaware of what had happened, so quietly had Magellan's men done their work. He was easily lulled into a false security when, upon hailing the *Victoria* as she passed, he was told by a member of the crew that Mendoza was below in his cabin.

All too late Quesada saw that he had been outwitted by Magellan, who now had three ships. The roles were reversed. The mutineers were the trapped ones.

That night, the three ships loyal to the Captain-General stretched their lengths across the harbor mouth, blocking the escape of the mutineers. Unfortunately, just before midnight, a storm of terrible fury broke upon them. Rain squalls, sleet and ice pelted the ships, obscuring all vision. Black scud whipped low over their mast-heads, while gales screamed through the rigging of the lonely ships.

Magellan knew that weather conditions, coupled with the dark, favored the escape of the *San Antonio* and the *Concepción*. He was sure that the mutineers would make the attempt to get clear of the harbor and abandon him. Once clear, they would flee back to Spain. Double watches were set. Of one thing however, Magellan was sure; the southerly direction of the gale was in his favor. It would make it extremely difficult for any vessel to wear out of the harbor against it. Coming in would be easy, but not going out.

It would require exceptional skill in seamanship plus a lot of luck to breast that gale, get clear of the capes, and out into the safety of the wide ocean waters. Magellan, with his old seaman's nose, sniffed the wind and with a wry smile asked for God's hand to rest upon him. Meanwhile, he judged the angles of the mutineers' ships upwind and figured that not all of God's elements favored the mutineers. He would be ready for any exigency.

It wasn't long before the rattle of anchor chains could be heard through the storm. But then the unexpected! Unable to make her tack against the gale and come about, the *San Antonio* came crashing

The San Antonio *came crashing down against the* Trinidad

down against the *Trinidad*. Magellan was prepared. With boarding irons and swords drawn, his crew tumbled aboard the fleeing ship, while from the opposite side, the little *Santiago* was able to maneuver down wind and board. In a few exciting moments of fierce battle the big *San Antonio* was forced to surrender. Captains Quesada and Cartagena were immediately put in chains.

The *San Antonio* was secured barely in time. For,

within the next few minutes, Magellan made out the dim outline of the *Concepción* screaming down the night wind toward them. She was on a desperate run for the sea and liberty. And now the *Trinidad,* with small rags of sails set in the storm, wheeled and blocked the *Concepción.* The wild crash of hulls, falling spars, and the screams of the rioters mingled with the deafening din of the gale.

The battle for the *Concepción* was on. But although there were a few sword cuts, bashed heads, and deep wounds, there was no loss of life. Magellan had secured the last of his mutinous traitors. On this lonely shore, on this dark night, he had felt, he believed, the helping hand of his Savior.

13

Retribution, cold and swift

Morning broke frosty and gray with some ice in the rigging. Winter was close at hand. And it must be remembered that south of the equator winter is the opposite of the northern winter. A cutting gale was still blowing, but the storm was breaking up. It was a chilled and subdued crew of seamen whom Ferdinand Magellan now held in his firm grip.

Punishment for the leaders of the revolt came

Magellan held a court-martial on the beach

quickly and with cruelty. Magellan, infuriated, held a brief court-martial on the beach in the morning. The trumpets blared, calling the court into session. The trial commenced. It was learned during the hearings that Captain Mendoza had actually been the instigator of the mutiny, and that Cartagena was the brain of it.

Directly supporting its leaders were seven officers and forty crewmen. The plot had been hatched entirely in Seville, prior to the sailing of the armada. This confirmed *Señor* Barbosa's warning letter. The worst offenders were the dead Mendoza, Quesada, Cartagena, and Juan Sebastian del Cano.

Cartagena, Quesada and del Cano were found guilty of treason. Magellan decreed that Quesada be immediately beheaded. Del Cano was put to work at hard labor on short rations, while Cartagena was condemned to be put ashore without food or water and left to starve to death at Port San Julien. Marooned with him, when the ships sailed, was Pedro Sanchez de la Reina, who in the meantime had tried to stir up another mutiny. Barring a miracle, theirs too was the death penalty.

Two points prevented the fair-minded Magellan from marooning the seven officers: first, lack of sufficient evidence, and secondly, the fact that the fleet desperately needed every available trained officer to assist in working the ships.

The forty guilty seamen were all severely flogged and placed in chains until after the ships sailed. In a sense, they were fortunate not to have been executed. The punishments were brutal, but had the mutineers succeeded, they would have murdered Magellan. With this heinous killing achieved, they would have robbed all mankind of the fruits of this great navigator's expedition.

Magellan, grim-faced and resolute, did in his

day only that which he felt imperative and justified to do in order to maintain discipline and security. He was the sovereign of his floating empire. As such it was his sacred duty to crush rebellion and keep the expedition moving forward to successful completion.

During the next few days at Port San Julien another dramatic and tragic event took place. The little *Santiago* was sent down the coast by Magellan on a minor exploring expedition. Its job was to search out two unknown bays and eliminate them as possible straits. Magellan wanted to make sure of every inch of this unexplored coast.

It was rocky, desolate, and dangerous. No man knew when his ship might encounter a jagged pinnacle rock, submerged only a few feet below the surface and not visible. The *Santiago* struck such a rock and quickly sank. Fortunately, all but one of the officers and crew were able to leap from the vessel's bowsprit to other rocks and thence to shore and safety. Later they were rescued by Magellan.

The loss of the *Santiago* was a blow to Magellan, but this was one of the hazards of such an expedition. And this was the reason why several ships were always needed. Uncharted coasts, unknown and ever-present perils of the deep were bound to bring disaster. Hence,

in those years it was never wise to invest all the hopes
of any expedition in one vessel.

As Magellan found out, the southern bays which the
Santiago had explored contained no straits. The weeks
wore on now, stretching into months. The Captain-
General was impatient to get along with his expedition
and to achieve his goal. His fleet had now been reduced
to four ships and his crews to fewer men. Sailing
southward, the armada was now well below Latitude
50 degrees south, where no known ship had ever been.

The end of the southern winter was near. Since leaving Port San Julien, the ships had encountered continuous storms, and the crews were wearied. Hence,
Magellan put in at a small bay he named Santa Cruz,
in what is now Patagonia. He wanted to explore all
the bays possible along his route. Riding into port on
the wings of a storm so vicious that it almost wrecked
his squadron, Magellan once more found a haven for
his ships in the Unknown World.

Here wood and fresh water were plentiful. Game
was abundant, too. Fishing was excellent. The harbor
water was sparkling clear, the beaches white and wind-
swept. So the Captain-General rested at anchor here
for two months in order to replenish his meat stocks
and to refresh his crews.

One day in Santa Cruz when some of the sailors on liberty were striding down the beach, they suddenly, and with great astonishment, came upon a giant savage. He was well over seven feet in height and of magnificent stature. The giant was unafraid of the crowd of seamen. His great teeth gleaming, he laughed and danced on the beach, throwing sand over his head in small clouds.

The sailors were amused and delighted with the friendly native. To show their own friendliness, they also danced on the beach and threw clouds of sand over their heads.

The giant's face was painted red, with half-moons drawn in blue under his eyes. Soon, other natives appeared. Due to the enormous size of these people, and because they possessed huge feet, Magellan named them *Patagones,* or the people of the big feet. One Patagonian was eventually lured on board the *Trinidad.* Once there, he was held captive to be carried back to Portugal for exhibition, although he put up a frightful struggle. On shore, the Patagonians were infuriated by the loss of their comrade.

The next day, a Spaniard in one of the liberty parties was struck by an arrow shot in revenge by a Patagonian. The Spaniard, struck in the thigh, drew the arrow from his flesh and started back to his boat. In a few moments, he fell forward on his face, dead. The arrow had been poisoned! This was the Europeans' first experience with a poisoned arrow.

In reprisal for the death of their shipmate, the Spaniards rushed ashore to kill Patagonians. But none could be found. Failing in this, they burned all their huts.

It was October now, the beginning of spring in these southern regions. Magellan wished to make full use of this advantage in his effort to locate the strait. His men were rested. His ships were replenished and in good order. Hence, he put out to sea at once with the armada.

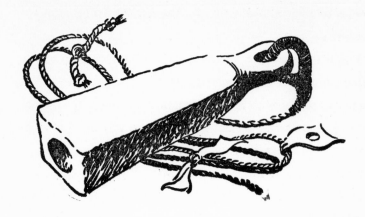

14

Test of a dream

Swinging south, the ships now sailed into what seemed a new world. Even the sea water beneath them held a strange gray-green lucidity. And while it was sunny, there was a sharp tang in the air that the men had never before experienced. Too, the ocean seemed to be "breathing off" a salty, pungent odor which was unfamiliar to them. This was caused by the presence of a species of microscopic sea life now known to abound in these waters.

The wind was not strong, but mountainous swells rolled smoothly under them. At times, between these great valleys of water, the ships became entirely lost to view. Some of the seamen became afraid and crossed themselves. At night the starry firmament was completely strange to them. The usual navigation stars had vanished to the north. Some frightened seamen declared that Magellan was a Satanic devil who was leading them off the edge of the world to their final doom.

Day after day they sailed the huge seas, onward, ever onward, while their dour-faced Captain-General paced his quarterdeck seemingly unconcerned.

Then, in a colorful cloud of sunset one evening, Magellan stared to the west and suddenly froze in his tracks. He glimpsed a cape. He named it the Cape of the Virgins, as the date was October twenty-first—a holy day named by the Catholics for St. Ursula and the Virgins. Magellan now reckoned his position as Latitude 52 degrees south. (Even with his crude instruments, his calculations are found today to be only a quarter of a degree in error because of his expert reckoning.)

Magellan now ordered his ships to follow him to the shore. Soon a great bay stretched before them. It was about five leagues in breadth, and faded off into the mists in the west. Magellan's heart pounded. The *Trinidad* was now the farthest south any known ship had ever been. But was this the bay for which he was searching?

The sun sank lemon-cold as the fleet reached closer to the coast. Enormous mountains, craggy, rocky, rose forbiddingly before them. The wind was icy and sharp. Just at twilight a fantastic mirage spread before the astonished sailors, showing all the jagged mountain peaks upside down. It was as if their own world was suspended in mid-air. It seemed to hang there, upside down, in the cold-yellow sunset. Even the huge swells of the sea looked as though they were rolling along, suspended in the heavens, all tinged with yellow!

Were they now entering between the gigantic walls of two worlds? Many were fearful. Even Magellan was awe-struck, but being a fearless man, he was completely enchanted. The Captain-General ordered the *San Antonio* and the *Concepción* to run inside the capes, explore the bay, and return to report their findings. His trusted Captain Barbosa in the *Victoria,* and he in the *Trinidad* would guard the entrance so that it would be blocked, and there would be no running back for Spain.

As the *Concepción* sailed into the bay, she seemed to be whirled about, as if caught by unseen phantom hands. Next, she vanished like a streak of lightning around the rocky cape. Soon the same phenomenon struck the *San Antonio*. It was breath-taking. But what was happening? Were the ships being sucked into some giant and hideous whirlpool?

Not on the next day, nor on the following was there any glimpse of the exploring vessels. Even the daring Magellan was consumed with foreboding for the possible loss of more men and more ships. But on the third evening the *San Antonio* appeared, suddenly. So suddenly that it seemed as if she were catapulted from some divine source. She hurtled out past the capes and was upon the *Trinidad* and *Victoria* in no time. Then, immediately behind her, in the same fashion, rushed the *Concepción*.

There was, it was learned, a forty-foot tide inside the capes, great whirlpools, and incredibly swift currents. At times, the currents reached over eight knots an hour. The *San Antonio* swept past, shooting off her bombards. As the smoke rose over the ships, Captain Mezquita of the *San Antonio* shouted out:

"The strait! The strait!"

The ships were called together and a conference of the officers was held on board the *Trinidad*.

"Inside the capes," stated Mezquita, "there are three huge bays. The most northwesterly of these bays, I am sure," he declared, "holds an opening to a western sea!"

There was a reverent silence for a moment among the officers as this statement was absorbed. Then Pilot Gomez of the *San Antonio* added his contribution:

"I am of the same opinion. But I say, let us strike a bargain. Now is the time for reason. We have now found this great strait. Let us be sensible and return to Spain while we are all alive, and there is yet time. For," cautioned Gomez, "if we strike bad fortune in the South Sea we shall all starve to death and leave our bones on that lonely ocean."

The resolute Captain-General struck his sun-bronzed fist on the cabin table with a resounding crash.

"We shall go forward!" he declared firmly. "I must see this strait first with my own eyes. And let me impress upon you one thing further. If we have to eat the leather on the yards, I will go on and on to discover what I have promised my king and our people. I have trust and faith that God will give us aid and good fortune!"

Gomez remained silent and sullen. The officers were then dispersed to their own ships. As the *Trinidad* led the way into the wide bay, the fleet followed. They sailed into a maze of channels and smaller bays leading off in dozens of different directions. Magellan tried this one and that one, but all led to dead ends and discouragement. Could his captains be mistaken after all?

Far to the northwest there loomed a towering cape of solid black rock. On all other sides were blue-white glaciers. Icy blasts of wind sent the little caravels careening onto their beam-ends in a smother of foam. High, unscalable crags, snow-covered and precipitous, towered above the mast-heads.

Beating up the narrow channels for some two weeks, the captains made hundreds of tacks through tortuous estuaries and great turbulent lagoons. The men caught their breaths as the icy blasts swept over the decks, while they worked halyards and braces with numb fingers. Magellan, feeling his way among the dangerous rocky channels, watched kelp sweeping down frothy-white currents that came from ahead.

The water, constantly being tested, was pure salt-sea

As the icy blasts swept over the decks, the

The omens were good, but if it existed, *where* was the unknown exit? There were so many islands and confusing channels that the Captain-General named the waters "The Bay of the Eleven Thousand Virgins." Confused by the countless estuaries and their blind endings, Magellan finally gave the order to anchor. Then provisioning a small, swift sailing boat from the *Trini-*

ships beat their way through the Strait

dad, he sent it out on an expedition for a week's exploring.

That night a terrible storm broke. It whipped the waters of their wild haven to a curdle. The *Trinidad* strained and groaned on her anchors, close under a precipitous cliff. Blinding flashes of lightning and deafening crashes of thunder rent the night, making it hideous. With the gray dawn there was no sign of the *Victoria,* nor the *Concepción,* nor the *San Antonio.* Magellan was torn with fearful foreboding. Had his ships foundered in that night of swirling storm and havoc?

On the fourth day there was still no word from the missing ships. However, the exploring longboat returned that noon. The pilots in the small boat stated that they had rounded the great cape to the northwest. Beyond this great cape, they declared, they saw the blue mists of a vast and peaceful ocean. This ocean, they further stated, spread off into infinity—as far as the eye could see.

Following their advice, Magellan moved carefully ahead with the *Trinidad,* through deep mountain gorges and rocky defiles. The channels, too, were strewn with pinnacle rocks. Barely would he have his sails squared onto a course when the lookout would warningly shout:

"Submerged rocks! Dead ahead! But all clear to larboard!"

And Magellan would give the command:

"Down helm! Hard a-lee! Jump to it, there!"

Then in a thunder of whipping canvas and crack of clews and rope-ends, the vessel would be hove down on her new course. Meanwhile, the leadsman would be continuing his sing-song calls:

"By the m-ark f-our! A quar-t-er l-ess s-ix!"

Magellan, every nerve taut, would listen for the warning of shallow water. Meanwhile the men waited like hounds at the tape, ready to spring into action to let everything fly—in time, they all hoped, to avoid crashing headlong into some deadly, unseen boulder lurking just below the surface. Magellan was happiest when the leadsman, swinging his great weight forward and dropping it into the depths, would shout out:

"No bottom!"

Then momentarily, all would relax, until the next warning came that the depths were decreasing again. It was a nerve-wracking and killing test of seamanship for all hands. But the veteran sailors did their jobs willingly and well.

The long streamers of brown kelp continued to float past them and go astern. After another week, Magellan reached the cape his pilots had seen. Magellan named this one *Deseado,* or the desired. While strange birds wheeled and screamed overhead, or were flung past, helpless on howling wind gusts from the mountains, Magellan strained for sight of what was ahead. Then, startlingly, there was a change in the wind direction! A softer wind seemed to caress the men's tired faces. They stared toward the new wind, which came from the west and almost dead ahead. Then the miracle happened!

The *Trinidad* sailed around the black, rocky cape and out onto a smooth Southern Sea that stretched for miles in every direction. Tears of joy streaming down his leathered cheeks, Ferdinand Magellan looked, then fell to his knees in prayer on the salt-caked deck of the *Trinidad*, and thanked God.

He had achieved the greatest accomplishment of any man of his day. His was the *first* ship to sweep into that great silent sea! His great dream was fulfilled. (He had found his strait!) He had discovered the long-sought-for South Sea, and the new route to the Spice Islands and the East. He had proven that the world could be circumnavigated!

Magellan ordered a bucket of pure sea water hoisted to the quarterdeck. Next, bringing a great cross on deck, and the royal standard of Old Spain, he dipped his hand in the crystal-clear water. He touched the holy cross, then the Spanish flag, and lastly his forehead, and declared:

"In the name of God, and King Charles of Spain, I name this sea the Pacific Ocean!"

15

A hard-won victory

Bombards were fired. The crews danced wildly around
the decks. The men hugged one another in ecstasy. But
Magellan? He was looking anxiously astern. Where
were his other three ships? What had happened to
them? Not one in sight! Returning under the lee of his
recently-named Cape Deseado, Magellan waited for
three harrowing days. During these days his crew
fished, or rested in the shelters of the ship. But occa-

sionally they would get up to peer through a sheltered gun port, or across a bulwark for some sight of the missing ships.

Then joyously one morning the *Concepción* appeared, sails tattered, and weather-beaten, but safe. There was a great rejoicing. Captain Serrano had been investigating the many southern channels for a possible exit to the South Sea. Then soon after him came the little *Victoria*, flying down channel with a similar story. She had been to the westward. But where was the *San Antonio?*

Together the three ships sailed back and forth, up and down the channels, probing, probing for their missing comrades, or any floating debris.

One night, as they sailed close to the shore, they observed several pinpoints of fire. These were brush fires beside which crouched fur-clothed savage peoples. Magellan named these natives *Fuegans* because of their many fires. And he called their land *Tierra del Fuego,* or the "Land of Fire."

It has been said since that these first Fuegans, now extinct, were the last of a great primitive race that had migrated all the way from Asia and were wrecked here. They had come perhaps ten thousand years before Magellan, but perished as a result of some plague as late as Magellan's time.

Even to the veteran seamen, this strange shore seemed like a "Never-Never World"—part of some forbidden "Beyond."

Captain Mezquita and the big *San Antonio* had vanished. No wreck or flotsam was seen. Magellan deemed it dangerous to delay longer. Their supplies were growing scanty. There was still so much distance to be covered.

So they sailed at once on the long voyage across the unknown and vast Pacific Ocean. Leaving signals and messages of the course on the beach for the *San Antonio* to follow, the *Trinidad, Victoria,* and *Concepción* sadly made their way past Cape Deseado. They headed across those thousands of miles of the great South Sea from which no man had ever brought any information.

Captain Mezquita on the *San Antonio,* however, unknown to his Captain-General, was no longer in command of his ship. The disgruntled Gomez had taken over and, perhaps hoping to feign the fate of the lost *Santiago,* sailed back for Spain.

The loss of the *San Antonio* was a crippling blow to

Magellan's fleet, as well as a dangerous threat to the security of the entire armada because she carried the major portion of their two years' supply of provisions.

On the arrival of the *San Antonio* in Spain, however, King Charles was incensed, openly declaring that he suspected treachery. He at once ordered the mutineers thrown into dungeons. And here within the dark and dank catacombs of Seville, these traitors languished through the long months ahead, awaiting the return of the great Magellan armada.

Meanwhile the fleet, on its second night at sea after leaving the Strait of Magellan, (as it later became known), was proceeding on its course with light variable winds. But the Captain-General was distracted from his duties by the shortness of rations caused by the *San Antonio's* foul desertion. While Magellan himself seemed to lead a charmed life immune to illness, he grieved for the intense suffering of his loyal men. His five-ship armada was now reduced to three vessels. His crew, due to losses, court-martials, and sickness, had decreased from two hundred and sixty-seven to one hundred and eighty-three men.

There were more than twelve thousand miles of lonely sea to traverse before they could be sure of provisions. But off beyond, somewhere there on the blue horizon, beckoned the fabulous Islands of Spice. What lay between? *Quien sabe?* Who could say?

For the next fifty-seven heartbreaking days the fleet sailed on, while food ran out and drinking water all but vanished. The flagship's chronicler, Pigafetta, commenting on the hardships at this point, wrote in his journal, "We ate biscuit, but in truth it was not biscuit, but powder full of worms; for the worms have devoured its substance. Then we were forced to eat the hides from the main booms which had covered parts of the booms and yards to prevent their chafing.

"These hides were so tough we were forced to tow them in the sea four or five days to soften them. Then we placed them over embers, toasted them and ate them. We also ate sawdust. Rats became such a delicacy that we paid a half a ducat (about a dollar) apiece to anyone catching them. Young mice were considered an even rarer delicacy."

Scurvy soon broke out, and the sailors died in great numbers. On this entire westward voyage no islands were seen. There were numberless islands passed, but always just barely over the horizon, and in all cases beyond view. Any one of them would have provided abundant food and water, but Magellan, of course, could not know this.

One morning, after some of their most horrible days at sea, a veteran quartermaster approached Magellan on the quarterdeck and begged that they go back to Spain, returning through their own westward straits. Only in this way, he pleaded, could the lives of the men be spared.

16

Tropical dilemma

Magellan, hearing the agonized moans of his suffering and dying seamen, was torn with grief. Even he was commencing to be dubious that they would ever reach shore now in time to save the expedition. But finally his old resolute will dominated the situation. He answered:

"Pray, my good man, for our deliverance. The way

home is nearly as far back as it is ahead. Surely we cannot now be far from land."

Again encouraged by their Captain-General, every man fell to his knees on deck and sent up his individual prayer. At dawn the following morning came a wild cheer from the lookout in the crosstrees:

"Land ho! Dead ahead! An island!"

There was wild rejoicing on the part of those who were able to move. Slowly the green bit of land on the horizon grew larger and took on form. By nightfall, they had come to anchor in a quiet tropical lagoon. On going ashore, however, they found that the island was of no value. It was only a small islet, coral fringed, with no drinking water, no fruits, and no habitation. Magellan named it "St. Paul."

Now even more subdued and more discouraged, the Captain-General and his men again sailed on. Six hundred miles farther on they encountered another group of islets, also proving barren. These the Captain-General named the "Tiburones," due to the prevalence of sharks in the region.

For three months and eight days, and through what seemed endless eternities of sailing, Magellan continued on before he finally sighted habitable land. But eventually he did come upon a large group of islands.

The Cebu islanders fled screaming to the green forests

Here the weary fleet came to anchor. Their haven was the island which is today known as Guam in the Marianas. And it was here that Gunner Andrew, the only Englishman with Magellan, died and was buried.

The natives on these islands endeavored to steal everything that they could lay hands on from the ships. When Magellan finally caught one group making off with his best longboat, this proved too great a strain for his patience. Infuriated, he opened fire on the village and destroyed most of it. Then, after every native had fled in terror to the forest, Magellan's men went on shore and obtained fresh fruits, vegetables, and water in abundant quantities and returned to their ships.

These supplies helped greatly to comfort the men who were sick and dying of scurvy, but unfortunately the provisions arrived too late for some. Many of the seamen were too ill to be able to eat the wondrous delicacies placed before them.

Thus, it is evident that the loss of the provisions on board the deserting *San Antonio* caused the death of the major portion of the personnel of the expedition, and almost caused the failure of Magellan's entire undertaking. But by now, of course, the men of the expedition had come to realize that nothing in the world could deter their Captain-General in his resolute ardor for a final victory. His motto, they said, was literally "Victory or Death!"

They felt confident, however, that because of his resolute spirit their great leader *would* see the expedition through to final success. Each hoped that he would be one of the men who would live through it all and who would, one fine day, walk up the main streets of Seville, gayly decorated in their honor.

Through calms and oily seas, long days of rain, and nights of misty stars, the fleet pressed on, ever and ever westward. At the island of Rota more food supplies were obtained, and at Samar another stop was made. Here, for ten days, the ships were overhauled and the crew given a chance to restore their spirits and health. At Limassawa, the next island they came upon, the explorers found the natives to be very friendly.

Then, about a month after the ships had left the Marianas, an emerald-green pinnacle rose out of the tropical seas. It proved to be the great island of Cebu, over three thousand feet in height. At last they had reached the East!

That night the three veteran ships drifted on a warm, light breeze into the quiet harbor of Opon, on the island of Cebu. This is one of a group of islands that later were named the Philippines. It was the first week of April, 1521. The armada had been gone from Spain more than a year and a half and had just concluded the longest sea passage in the history of the maritime world.

Magellan raised the holy cross on board the *Trinidad*. Religious services were held. All dropped to their knees, and with their Captain-General leading them in prayer, every man thanked God for their miraculous deliverance and asked comfort for the sick and dying. Bombards were fired. Every flag and banner on board was hoisted in celebration.

On shore, the native Cebu islanders were at first terror-struck by the explosions of the cannon. They fled screaming to the green forests. After a time, however, they recovered their courage and, spurred by curiosity, returned to the harbor-front to stare at the great Spanish ships, the largest they had ever seen.

But these great ships, resting there with their cannons pointing at them—were they friends? Or were they enemies who came to destroy them? They gazed at the huge Cross of St. James on the sail of the flagship. It was impressive. Where had these strangers with their enormous white-winged vessels come from? Perhaps from heaven?

Curiosity soon overwhelmed them, and a welcoming party ventured out to the flagship. They were received, of course, in all friendship. The natives were dressed in silk robes and fine jewels. Several interpreters accompanied the boarding party, and through them it was learned that the islanders had brought greetings from the King of Cebu, and an invitation to Magellan and his officers to come ashore. There they were to be received with the highest possible honors by the island King.

Magellan accepted on the condition that first, all his sick and ailing men would be removed to shore, administered to, and comforted. This was agreed upon. As soon as these duties had been accomplished, and all the sick men were transported ashore, Magellan, with his captains and pilots, landed on the foreign beach. Here the Captain-General planted the cross and declared:

"In honor of Philip, the son of King Charles V, of Spain, I do hereby declare these islands to be the royal property of the King of Spain and his great people!"

Soon surrounded by many officials in bright vestments, Magellan and his men were asked to go to the palace of the King. Subsequently, in great pomp and panoply the great procession moved on. There was a merry, musical clanging of cymbals, the beating of kettle-drums, and the skirl of bagpipes which the Spaniards had never heard before. Many of the musical instruments, Magellan learned later, had been imported from Old Cathay and the Islands of Spice.

In such impressive gayety, the victorious Spanish explorers were escorted to the royal island palace.

The natives along the byways, Magellan noted, were nearly naked, but the aristocrats wore richly adorned robes covered with jewels of great splendor. Within the palace there were bamboo-latticed windows. From here one commanded a magnificent vista of the harbor entrance and the sea beyond. The King strode forward. He was short, heavy-set and muscular. His skin was swarthy, and his black hair fell nearly to his shoulders. Bright golden earrings hung from his ears.

Around his neck he wore a golden collar set with glistening gems. He wore a loin cloth beneath his bright robe. His broad chest was enscrolled with flowering tattoo marks, and was bare for coolness; but from his shoulders he wore a handsome red robe surmounted with etchings of shining gold. Wrapped around his head was a turban of finely spun veiling set with many tiny jewels.

After greeting his friends, the King sat on his throne of richly carved tropical woods. He was surrounded by a large assemblage of his court, both men and women. The women were attractively dressed in many-colored silks. As the warm tropical winds swept in from the sea, and the faint melodies of the strange island music drifted over them, Magellan and his men felt a wondrous enchantment in their newly found paradise.

The Captain-General, through one of his interpreters, then explained to the island monarch that he represented the greatest monarch and the greatest nation on earth, Spain. In spite of the enormous distance, he had come all the way from Spain to bring to the King of Cebu, he said, greetings from his king. He also wished to trade, he stated, and to offer the people a new enlightenment in religion which would brighten their lives.

The King of Cebu, who was called rajah by his people, replied that the Spanish were welcome on his island, and that he would be happy to trade with them. He could not make any promises about the religious purpose of the visit, although he did wish to know more about their system for enlightenment. First, however, the King reminded the Spaniards that they must pay harbor and custom fees, as was the routine procedure for all incoming ships.

Magellan replied that his king paid tribute to no nation, and that the Spaniards had come as friends, but if the king was going to make hostile demands upon them, then they were prepared for war. A Siamese trader who was the guest of the rajah whispered to him that he believed Magellan was of a great Portuguese expeditionary force, and advised the rajah to use caution.

Magellan understood the interpretation, and overhearing the statement, interposed: "My king is even more powerful than the Portuguese king. He is the King of Spain, and Emperor of the whole Christian World."

The rajah, then thinking further, replied:

"Very well. You are now officially received in the port as my guests. Let this talk of business be forgotten. Let us banquet and enjoy our mutual companionship."

With this friendly ultimatum, great bowls of fruits, bananas, figs, coconut, rice, eggs, meats, and many wondrous things were brought in. An enormous feast was held. Magellan and his men ate joyously to the accompaniment of sweet music, and were entertained by groups of gayly veiled, laughing dancing girls.

Following the impressive banquet, Magellan and his ship's officers were invited to spend the night in the great palace of the rajah, where they slept the good sleep of tired victors. Their bodies and their very bones ached from their long and terrible struggle with the sea.

17

A tropic tomb

After the Captain-General and his men had rested for a couple of days, Magellan was impatient to hold religious services, with interpreters, so that the islanders could learn of Christianity. From the ships, meanwhile, a portion of his men were transporting trade goods ashore to a warehouse. Here the Spanish planned to establish a permanent trading station with the natives.

Magellan himself was searching out a spot suitable for religious services. A huge holy cross was brought ashore and placed on a high knoll in the town. It was here that the great explorer, a few days later, explained all the wonders and advantages of Christianity to his friends of Cebu.

Magellan persuaded the rajah to burn all his wooden idols and to embrace Christianity. This the King of Cebu did. Not only that, he also accepted Christianity and convinced his own people of the advantages of doing likewise.

The rajah was overjoyed in the new-found happiness of the creeds adopted from the Spaniards. Their spiritual meanings, he felt, were beautiful. Hence, the King of Cebu and Magellan became close friends with this new spiritual bond between them. And Magellan was happy that his stay at Cebu was successful. His ambitions expanded. He perhaps acquired too much confidence. He was impatient to visit neighboring islands in order to spread the sphere of influence of Christianity. As soon as this was achieved, he told himself, he would sail for the Islands of Spice. Then he would return to Spain. Thus he would complete his circumnavigation of the world.

Already by reaching the East through the newly-

found strait, he had accomplished what no man before
him had ever done. But the lovely green island of Mactan lay beckoning just north of Cebu. He wished to
bring the peoples of this island into Christianity too.
Mactan was separated from Cebu by only a mile-wide
channel. Rumors had reached Magellan that the rajah
of this lesser island was rebellious to the idea of Christianity. This was a challenge. He wished no island in
his path to remain barren of the fruits of enlightenment.

The King of Cebu understood Magellan's zeal and
sympathized with it. He too desired that the rajah of
Mactan and his people should espouse Christianity.
He advised Magellan that if the Captain-General would
send armed Spaniards to his assistance, he would engage
and subjugate his rival rajah. To his friend, the King
of Cebu, Magellan replied:

"I thank you for your offer of assistance, but I have
no desire to involve you in a civil war with your own
people. I shall go alone, with a few picked men, and
bring your rival rajah into Christianity. I shall also
show him what happens to those who seek to flaunt the
authority of a royal edict!"

Magellan's own officers tried to dissuade their Captain-General from attempting a warlike venture against

Swarming down to the surf, the jungle warriors

this island with its large population. They did not wish
to see their heroic leader imperil his life on such a rash
adventure—perhaps an overzealous one. Magellan, however, replied to their entreaties:

"As a good pastor I am obligated to shepherd all of
my flock."

In addition, through the boldness which marked all
of the Captain-General's decisions, he again stated to
his own men:

"I not only will go to subjugate this recalcitrant ra-

soon overwhelmed Magellan's little band

jah, I shall go only with our own Spanish soldiers. I will prove to him that we, with our invincible arms, can conquer any of our enemies who refuse to submit to the authority of the King of Spain."

The very next morning, in late April of 1521, Ferdinand Magellan sailed with his fleet across the coral-green channel to Mactan. Here he sent word ashore demanding the surrender of the rajah of Mactan to the authority of the King of Spain and the King of Cebu. The rajah not only refused, he challenged the Spaniards to come and try to subdue him.

Magellan next endeavored to maneuver his little fleet close enough inshore to bombard the village with cannon. Coral reefs and other obstructions in the channel unfortunately prevented this. Unable to make use of cannon was a catastrophic handicap. Still undaunted, Magellan in an unusually brash decision landed in the surf with only forty-nine trusted soldiers armed with arquebuses and swords.

On this strange foreign shore, in water up to their thighs, struggling over rough and jagged coral, Magellan and his small staff opened fire. While attacking, they were plunging on for the dry beach. They were immediately set upon by more than a thousand Mactan jungle warriors. Using their long, dreadful lances, and firing poisoned arrows from giant blow-guns, they started to surround the Spanish landing party.

Magellan divided his men into two companies, with his musketeers on one side, and the cross-bow men on the other. A blistering and savage barrage of ball-and-musket was gallantly waged for more than an hour. The explosions and flashings of the arquebuses at first greatly frightened the island fighters. So, too, did the astounding number of their dead.

However, when the natives discovered that some of

their plain wooden lances were penetrating what they had believed to be the sacred armor that the Spaniards wore, they immediately became emboldened to rasher advances. It was soon thereafter that the jungle warriors launched a raging attack into the surf. Swarming down in enormous numbers, they soon overwhelmed Magellan's little band.

The brave Captain-General received a lance in his forehead which knocked him over backward into the surf. During the next few moments, several poisoned arrows pierced his body. His death was now a certainty. Quickly realizing the hopelessness of his plight, the gallant commander, dark eyes rolling piteously with suffering, ordered his men to leave him and flee for their lives.

All too easily abandoning their heroic Captain-General, the remaining Spaniards formed a retreating wedge and fled through the scarlet waters to their waiting boats. As soon as the Spanish soldiers were a safe distance away, a vicious horde of the islanders fell upon the already mortally wounded Magellan to complete their hideous task. Only eight Spanish soldiers eventually reached their vessels alive. The rajah of Mactan had won a complete victory! Magellan was dead.

18

Confusion in the fleet

This terrible disaster was, at first, unbelievable to the
men of Magellan's armada. Their Captain-General
killed in action? It just couldn't be! But the mortal
body of their proud leader was lifeless. His heroism, his
sacrifices for others, and his deeds would become im-
mortal. Crushed by the tragic loss of their commander,
saddened, and sick with failure, the Spaniards silently

sailed back to Cebu to reorganize their plans and to de-
cide upon a new leader.

The King of Cebu, on learning of Magellan's death,
professed profound grief. Yet all of the Cebu islanders,
including the King, seemed more affected by the fact
that the white commander, who they thought was invincible, had so ignominiously succumbed to a simple
death, just as easily as could any of their own common
brown savages.

In short, the "invincible white man," and the
Spaniards in particular, had suffered a tremendous loss
of "face" and prestige in the Tropics. To all of the
islanders and the rajahs it was an astounding discovery.
Added to this was the fact that the overwhelmed Span-
iards never sought revenge for their murdered leader.
Nor has this phase ever been satisfactorily explained.
To this day, it remains a mystery.

A feeble offer, it seems, was made to the rajah of
Mactan to ransom the body of Magellan. But the rajah
contemptuously refused to give up this rare treasure
of war, so victoriously obtained. Beyond this, nothing
further was attempted by the subdued Spaniards.

They appeared completely frustrated by the absence
of their great leader. The only possible explanation for

their lack of action was the demoralized condition of the men after their long grueling voyage. They were eager to reach their homeland as fast as possible. And whatever became of the mortal remains of the great leader is even today a mystery.

The officers and men of the fleet now held a conference. First, they must elect a new leader. Strangely enough, after making so many remarks about the fact that Magellan was Portuguese and not a Spaniard, they elected another Portuguese as their leader. The commander who would lead them forward on their last, long passage home was one of the fleet's navigators, Odoardo Barbosa.

Second in command, and the armada's chief navigator, was Juan Serrano, Magellan's closest and oldest friend in the fleet. When their final roll call of all hands was taken, it was discovered that the entire personnel consisted of only one hundred and fifty-six officers and men. The tragic toll of the expedition stood at one hundred and eleven men, and two ships.

It was decided to remove at once all the trade goods located in the warehouse ashore, and prepare for sea. A shore party to recover these goods was headed by Juan Serrano with twenty-seven loyal men. Among these was Juan Lopes Carvalho, who was pilot in charge of the boat. As soon as the boats landed, they were surrounded by several scores of islanders who purportedly were going to escort them safely to the warehouse.

On a given signal, however, the natives suddenly fell upon the Spaniards with kris and spear. Caught unprepared and surprised, the Spaniards in a few moments were whittled to bits. Carvalho and one other sailor escaped, only because they were guarding the landing boat and able to row swiftly away. These two fled back to the ship with the announcement of another massacre!

Obviously, the prestige of the Spaniards had now dropped so low that even the Cebu islanders would not support them as friends. It is believed that if the Spaniards had made a truly valiant attempt to attack Mactan, or to retrieve their lost leader in some forceful manner, the Cebu islanders would have recognized these moves as showing courage, and would not have perpetrated this last foul slaughter.

Be this as it may, the Spaniards, after suffering a further loss of men, now lifted anchors and sailed ignominiously away. At this point, Juan Lopes Carvalho was placed in command. He was deposed after three months, however, and the crew elected Gonzalo de Espinosa as his successor.

The Concepción *was burned and scuttled*

It was still the intent of all who remained to reach the Islands of Spice. Only in this way could Magellan's great plan for the complete circumnavigation of the world be realized. And this, they recognized, was the edict of their king. Sailing on west, the three ships touched at the Island of Palawan, one of the Philippine Group. Here they provisioned with pigs, poultry, bananas, and rice, and took a supply of fresh water.

As the *Concepción* was now leaking badly, they de-

cided to abandon her here. In addition, all three ships
were now scantily manned. With one ship less, they
would be able to concentrate their working power. So,
after transferring men and provisions, the *Concepción*
was burned and scuttled in the Sulu Sea. The remaining
two ships, the *Trinidad* and *Victoria,* sailed from
Palawan on June 21, 1521.

The two ships proceeded across the Celebes Sea and
made a stop at Borneo. Here they picked up a native
pilot who would take them through the treacherous
reefs of the Molucca Sea.

It was in November that they finally arrived at the
armada's much-sought-for Islands of Spice, the Moluc-
cas. Specifically, they landed at the island of Tidore, of
the Ternate Group, now part of the Dutch East Indies.
Here all of the men again dropped to their knees on
the decks of their ships and thanked the Almighty for
completing another link in Magellan's great vision of
achievement. The armada had now, for the first time
in world history, completed the circle of ships sailing
around the world, because other Spanish ships coming
from around Africa had already reached Ternate.

The two ships fired their artillery and there was
great celebrating. While in Tidore, the men received
the news that Magellan's old friend, Francisco Serrano,

was dead. It was here, too, that they were warned that King Manuel of Portugal was still seeking revenge against Magellan. He had heard through his spies that the Captain-General with his victorious armada was en route home. Subsequently, he had dispatched a fleet with heavy cannons to intercept the Spanish armada, capture Magellan, and destroy his fleet.

Captain Del Cano, who had been given command of the *Victoria,* decided to give a wide berth to the Portuguese possessions along the homeward route, as a safety precaution. On the other hand, he was told that the King of Spain had sent out his fleet looking for his friend Ferdinand Magellan in order to give him safe escort home. Forewarned, and with these facts in hand, Del Cano sailed from the Islands of Spice in December, 1521.

Dangerous leaks were now commencing to develop in the hull of the *Trinidad,* and it finally became unsafe for her to remain at sea. Perforce then, Magellan's proud old flagship, with fifty-four of her men on board, had to give up the hard fight to return home to Spain. Sadly she made farewell signals to the little *Victoria,* and headed back for Ternate.

Here the glorious ship which had carried her heroic Captain-General through every conceivable strife and storm found her last haven. Eventually, she was captured by the Portuguese, wrecked and left to disintegrate among the coral waters of the great Molucca Sea, not far from where her own great commander had met his end.

19

Furtive flight

It was now late spring of the year 1522. The hardy little *Victoria,* the last survivor of the noble Captain-General's fleet, had beaten her way eastward across the vast, heat-riven Indian Ocean. As they passed close to Mozambique, a Portuguese colony, the men were sorely in need of water. It was imperative that they make some port swiftly. Too, they had a virulent tropical fever aboard as a result of which they had already consigned twenty-one men to the deep.

Fear of capture by the Portuguese, however, finally prevented Captain Del Cano from taking so great a risk at this last and precious stage of their home-ward passage. But early in July their provisions and water became so alarmingly scarce that a decision was forced upon him. It was now a matter of life or death. They simply must make port for food and water.

By now, however, they had breasted the Indian Ocean. They had fought a fierce fight of gales, hail, and sleet in working around the Cape of Good Hope. Wearied, suffering from fever, hunger, thirst, and afflicted with anemia, they discovered themselves to be close to the Portuguese Cape Verde Islands. The original crew of the *Victoria* that had stepped aboard at Seville numbered fifty-five, but now their total was only nineteen.

They had been absent from their homes nearly three years. This, then, was the small, emaciated crew that sailed into the Cape Verdes, desperately seeking water, food, and comfort for their sick and suffering. Captain Del Cano, well aware of the awful risk involved in entering a Portuguese port, concocted a false story. Sending a boat ashore with rice for payment, he instructed the pilot to declare to the Portuguese that Magellan with two ships had already gone on ahead.

Magellan, the pilot was instructed to say, should now be nearing the coast of Spain. The *Victoria,* thus, was feigning to be a laggard. At first the Portuguese were inclined to believe the tale. Meanwhile the *Victoria's* longboat was filled with provisions purchased with precious rice. Their water barrels were filled. But the men were shaky and in fear of capture. Fatigued and ill, it was impossible for them not to show their anxiety. Their hands trembled as they loaded their supplies. Their faces twitched in fear, and their eyes were nervous.

The wily Portuguese could not mistake the signs. They became suspicious of the story given them. Picking one of the weakest of the seamen, they sneaked him away from his shipmates. Bribing him with some rare and delicious brandy, they finally persuaded him to betray his comrades with the true story. But the men in the boats immediately discovered the absence of their shipmate, and knowing his weakness for spirits, feared betrayal.

Hastily casting off, leaving their miserable mate behind, they fled with foaming oars back to the *Victoria*. Captain Del Cano, seeing their frantic haste, sensed at once what was wrong. Leaping to his halyards and braces, he vigorously prepared his ship for instant flight to sea as soon as his men could get alongside. With anchor weighed, and bearing off on a fair wind, the *Victoria* circled gently around, grabbing her water, provisions, men, and finally her longboat on the run.

Then, squaring away on the fair wind, the little *Victoria* pressed on every inch of canvas that she could raise. Coming not far behind her longboat were half a dozen swift Portuguese caravels. Raising their sails with abandon, slipping their anchors in frantic manner, they were squaring around downwind after the fleeing Spaniards with an eye to their capture.

The chubby *Victoria,* under seventy feet in length and leaking badly, was dragging from her hull long streamers of seaweed, barnacles, and various sea growths that made her sluggish. Her sails were tattered and did not draw well. So weary and so late, would she now be captured by the dread Portuguese? King Manuel, still thirsting for revenge, they all knew, would pay handsomely for this treasure, the Spanish *Victoria!* Anything to prevent the heroic Magellan expedition from victoriously completing its glorious triumph! Anything to blemish the proud name of Magellan!

But soon after the longboat was hoisted on board, the *Victoria* commenced gaining on her pursuers. Some said they felt the very breath of Magellan himself puffing from astern, slowly blowing them foot by dreadful foot out of the reach of the frightening caravels. Magellan was still with them in spirit! The Portuguese found themselves just split-seconds too slow to thwart the escape of their coveted prize.

After the *Victoria* had passed the dreaded capes and was well out to sea, an astounding discovery was made. On the Portuguese shore the day was Thursday, while on the ship it was only Wednesday! The faithful chronicler Pigafetta checked and re-checked his journal from front to rear, from rear to front, again and again. Captain Del Cano checked his log book. But definitely, on board it was Wednesday; it *had* to be Wednesday!

What had happened? Again, aboard, a final check was made. Without skipping any pages, day after day, the journals had been faithfully maintained, each succeeding day placed after the previous one. They could not possibly have missed a day! But where had it vanished? They were the *first* to discover that he who counters against the earth in her rolling course will gain a full day upon completing a circumnavigation of the globe. Not even Prince Henry the Navigator, Columbus, nor even the famed Ruy Faleiro had been aware of this startling fact.

That night on board the weather-beaten *Victoria* all gave thanks for the arrival of nightfall with its welcome mantle of darkness and for the fact that the horrid Cape Verde Islands were lost to view beyond their sterns.

Del Cano knew that word of their presence in the Cape Verdes and of their homeward route for Spain had leaked out. Would the vengeful Portuguese with their fresher and faster ships still be able to overtake them? Time alone would give the answer. At night, not a single light was shown, not even running lights as the *Victoria* lurched wearily homeward. Each morning as dawn broke, the horizon was clean-swept; not a

sign of a sail anywhere! Praise to God! Praise to God
in His Heaven!

The vessel was now leaking badly. In fact she was
leaking so badly that every man aboard had a continuous round of labors at the pumps. Even so, there were
times when it was doubted that the pumps could keep
up with the inflowing sea. The seamen, staggering to
their knees after but a little sleep, would bend again
and again at the long handles of the pumps in seemingly endless work to stave off death by sinking.

It was at this point that Captain Del Cano wrote
in his log book: "The men are feebler than living
men have ever been before." Such was their plight
at dawn one morning in early September, 1522,
when the lookout from the crow's nest hoarsely cried
down to the bleached decks:

"Ahoy there on deck! Land ho! Dead ahead!"

They had sighted the craggy heights of Cape Saint
Vincent! Trembling with exhaustion, some of the men
sent up quavering cheers. Others dropped to the decks
in silent prayers. God be praised! God be praised!
Europe at long, long last! Fascinated, men stumbled
toward their gunwales, hung on with shaking muscles,
and stared at the unbelievable apparition of the long

coastline before them. Rubbing their sore and tired eyes, again and again they looked, just to make sure!

In another day and night they glimpsed the break on the blue horizon which every man recognized to be the mouth of the great Guadalquivir River and Seville.

20

Home at last!

As the weathered *Victoria* entered Seville, she fired her entire battery of cannons. And as her salvos echoed over the rooftops and down through the narrow streets, the people rushed to the harborside, as they had when the *San Antonio* came back. When the smoke rose into the golden morning sun, men, women, and children, with tears of gladness wetting their cheeks, shouted:

"Look! It's the *Victoria* come home!" Then more and longer cheers of, *"Viva* Victoria! *Olé* Victoria! *Bravo,* Magellan!"

Flags and banners were hoisted quickly. Soon they were flying from everywhere. Then came shouts of:

"Is my Pancho on board? Is Luiz safe? How about León?"

More tears. . . . More saddened faces. Of the two hundred and sixty-seven seamen who had left on five proud ships three years before, only two ships had returned home, this one with but nineteen survivors!

As the *Victoria* was affectionately moored to her quay, cathedral bells tolled for the missing ones. These melodies echoed and re-echoed across the heights of the red-roofed city, and along the white banks of the ancient Guadalquivir, seeming to spell out in sad murmurings the names of all those missing. They seemed to be saying over and over again, "Magellan's fleet is home! Magellan's dream is realized! The world has been circumnavigated for the first time! See, the brave circumnavigators are home! They are home, at last!"

Lacking only a few weeks, the expedition had been absent three whole years. Within this time they had voyaged over 43,000 miles! A record for history! A vast assemblage was flocking to the quay and gathering around the veteran ship. The *Victoria* home! All wished to pay homage. The greatest, the most wonderful event in all the world was taking place. "How fortunate we are to be witnessing it now!" But it was with choking throats and fast-beating hearts that the throngs watched Juan Sebastian del Cano and his haggard men come stumbling down the creaking gangway.

Others gazed at the proud *Victoria* with all her banners flying. Not a trace of the rich yellow paint was left on her hull. Gone was the gold on her once-bright figurehead. Her resplendently yellow sails, too, were faded and mildewed. The great Cross of St. James was barely discernible in outline. The planks in the bleached hull were warped and leaky. But, there she was! Yes, there she rode! Truly, it was incredible!

Captain Del Cano and his skeleton-like shipmates staggered and weaved as they moved along the quay! It was as if the quay itself were the heaving, rolling sea. They only managed to steady themselves by holding onto the hand-ropes along the quay. "God bless them! What privations they must have suffered for their great ambition!"

They were barefoot. Their clothes, such as they

wore, had faded, and were but rags. But their faces bore
the wrinkles and kisses of foreign suns. "Such brave
mariners! God bless them!"

The people surged forward. "And the wonderful
Ferdinand Magellan, how is *he?*" As the sad news
of the death of their great Captain-General reached
them, a silence settled over the crowd. "Ferdinand
Magellan dead? What a grievous loss!"

To think that the brilliant Magellan, and his loyal
friend, Ruy Faleiro, the two greatest heroes of circumnavigation, were absent! *"Vale* Magellan! Godspeed Magellan! *Vale* Faleiro! Godspeed Faleiro!
Assuredly they are together now, in heaven, watching
this expedition being received by their loved ones.
But you others here, come into our homes. Take rest."
The men looked at their loyal friends gratefully, but
murmuring, "Not yet."

First they must go to their little chapel-by-the-sea,
of *Señora de la Barrameda,* and give fervent thanks
to the Almighty for their deliverance. The men fell to
their knees on the ancient cobbles and kissed the be-
loved stones. Nor did they try to hold back the tears
that rushed to their glad eyes. Home at last! What a
boon! What a blessing!

A soft hush fell over the crowd. Finally the little band of nineteen barefoot wanderers got up, and shuffled off toward the chapel. As they passed, the people touched their garments reverently and murmured blessings. Some stared as if the returned seamen were ghosts out of the tomb. "Completely around the world they have been, and for the first time!" It was repeated, unbelievably, over and over again, and yet again.

"The sea can no longer be the same hideous place of perils that it once was. Magellan has proved it. The fleet of his dreams has sailed around the earth from east to west! Fire the bombards! Hoist the flags!"

"God bless Magellan and his dream!" His great expedition had found the strait and had blazed a new route to the Spice Islands and Old Cathay!

The vast, unknown South Sea had been crossed and named the Pacific by Magellan. New stellar constellations had been found and charted. Great strides had been made in calculating the shape and size of the earth. For the first time a true gauge of longitude and of the manner in which it should be reckoned was realized.

New lands had been discovered and annexed for

the power and glory of Spain. Christianity and enlightenment had been widely spread among savage peoples.

"Vale Magellan! *Bravo* Magellan!"

21

Magellan the victor

The *Victoria* brought home in her holds such rare spices as cinnamon, mace, ginger, curry, tarragon, paprika, peppercorns, cacao, and nutmeg. Also precious sandalwood. The cargo of this one small ship, valued at over $100,000, more than paid the expenses of the entire expedition!

But the real values of Magellan's achievements were not in products, nor in the gold and silver that the ship brought home. They were in the precious and priceless treasures of knowledge and enlightenment which made not only Spain but the whole world richer.

But on shore in Seville at this time, a handful of men were quaking in their small and anxious souls. These were the traitors from the *San Antonio,* the leaders of the terrible mutiny at Port San Julien. Most of them were still in the dungeons where they had been flung by King Charles who was so loyal to Magellan. But the sad news of the death of their brave Captain-General cheered the black hearts of the mutineers and gave them hope for freedom.

The returning seamen from the *Victoria* hesitated to bring charges against their former shipmates because they knew that their own captain, Juan Sebastian del Cano, was also seriously implicated in the mutiny. And Captain Del Cano *had* completed the circumnavigation of the globe begun by Magellan and *had* brought the *Victoria* home from the Philippines. For this final accomplishment he and his shipmates were rewarded.

Each one of the blackguards, however, except Del Cano, was destined soon to fade into oblivion. As an accomplice, Del Cano himself was forced to destroy all possible evidence of the mutiny, and to aid in the actual freeing of the mutineers in the dungeons, or himself be hanged. Hence he destroyed Magellan's diary and many other precious documents of the great voyage. For these papers would surely have convicted him for the traitor that he was. The loss of these papers deprived the world of the most treasured chronicles of the expedition.

And so it was that even after Ferdinand Magellan's tragic death, at the age of only forty-one years, his enemies were still trying to wash the awful guilt from their hands. But they were never entirely successful. Years later when the *Trinidad* was captured by the Portuguese and wrecked by them in the Far East, the timbers of this grand ship disgorged, as if in vengeance, some of Magellan's personal papers. They proved the unsavory facts of the voyage, and flung out into the open the truth of the dread mutiny at Port San Julien.

The great Spanish chronicler, Antonio Pigafetta, was also forced, for a long time, under penalty of death, to maintain a stilled tongue about the mutiny. This anxiety, though, rankled deeply with one so loyal to Magellan. He wrote in his journal: "I hope that the renown of so high-spirited a captain will never be forgotten. Among the many virtues which adorned him, one was especially remarkable—he always remained calm and steadfast, even amid the greatest misfortune.

"He bore the pangs of hunger more patiently than did any of us. There was no man alive who understood more about the science of cartography and navigation. The truth of this is proved by the way he brought to light things that no man before him had ever adventured to see, nor to discover."

Thus, the startling and awful truths of the Port San Julien mutiny eventually were uncovered to the world in two ways. First, by the unexpected discovery of Magellan's documents from his sunken flagship. Secondly, by facts pieced together in later years from confessions by members of the crews, also from Pigafetta himself when he was an old man.

It was destined that the world should know of the terrible obstacles Magellan had been forced to overcome, and the treachery of the men whose disloyalty nearly caused the destruction of one of the world's most important scientific explorations and achievements.

Throughout his entire life Magellan's achievements were constantly made difficult by the ignorant, the selfish, and the jealous. He was a forced outcast even from his own country. So it remains the heritage of the living to pay homage to this great man. He never reached home to receive the rich garlands of glory awaiting him. But the whole world received the blessings of his work and the glories of his learning.

Today, and forevermore in the years to come, just north of the foam-white crags of stormy Cape Horn, his great Strait glorifies his name. And beyond his Land of Fire, in stellar splendor, drift the Magellanic Clouds, brilliant star clusters in the soft, southern firmament. They are always there to remind us of the now long-gone swaying mast-heads of Magellan's armada struggling across that vast unknown sea, the Pacific Ocean.

And off there beyond beyond, as well as in the hearts of all men everywhere, there is raised a symbol of heroic courage, the ideal to serve unselfishly a great cause for mankind. That symbol is the fine and the proud name of Ferdinand Magellan.

"Bravo Magellan! *Vale* Magellan!"

Index